Telecommunication Agreements for Commercial Buildings

What Every Real Estate Lawyer Should Know

Ajay Raju

Section of Real Property, Probate and Trust Law

Defending Liberty
Pursuing Justice

Cover design by ABA Publishing

08 07 06 05 04 5 4 3 2 1

Library of Congress Cataloging-in-Publication Data
Raju, Ajay.
    Telecommunication agreements for commercial buildings / Ajay Raju.
    p. cm.
    ISBN 1-59031-573-1
    Telecommunication—Law and legislation—United States. 2. Contracts for work and labor—United States. 3. Commercial buildings—Law and legislation—United States. I. Title.

KF2765.R35 2005
343.7309'94—dc22   2005030604

CONTENTS

CHAPTER 4

Installation and Commissioning   43

CHAPTER 5

Liability, Indemnification and Insurance   65

ACKNOWLEDGMENTS

This book was not written in a vacuum. A number of people contributed to its success. My mentor and good friend, Bob Lane, who turned nebulous drafts into a highly polished manuscript, deserves special thanks and acknowledgment. My treasured and irreplaceable secretary, Nancie Lucera, deserves special praise for bearing the load of endless deadlines. My former intern, Filip Mielczak, offered exceptional research assistance. My good friends, Joe Tuso, Susanna Randazzo, Eric Diaz, John Ferer, and Niraj Patel, offered valuable suggestions on several portions of the manuscript. My parents, and their children, Pamela, Vijay, and Sonia, and their grandchildren, Madison, Genevieve, and Jake, humble me daily with their unconditional support, love, and encouragement. Lastly, my editors at the ABA, especially Christopher Hanback and Jeffrey Barnes, provided ongoing support and encouragement without which this book would not have been possible.

CHAPTER I

Closing the Last Mile Gap

The Demand for Broadband Communications

Demand for high-speed Internet access and data-intensive broadband communications services has grown exponentially in recent years due to the dizzying pace of technological innovations, a competition-friendly regulatory environment, and the increased acceptance of and interest in the Internet. Accompanying this insatiable demand and, in many cases, providing the impetus for the technological innovations that fuel it, is the ubiquitous nature of communications-dependent applications that our modern society depends upon to unlock communications barriers and to facilitate the timely and accurate flow of information.

Over the past decade, the growing spectrum of telecommunications offerings, resulting from and, created by, rapidly evolving advances in technology, the world-wide endorsement of free enterprise, a regulatory push for a competitive landscape and the globalization of modern commerce, have increased our modern society's appetite for, and dependence upon, communications-dependent applications. For example, prior to 1995, businesses used the Internet primarily to exchange electronic mail and to occasionally surf the World Wide Web. Since then, the explosive growth in the development and use of the Internet has resulted in a quantum leap in business and recreational activities that depend upon Internet communications. It has now become common for businesses and consumers to buy and sell products and services via the Internet, surf Web pages featuring animated graphics, transmit audio and streaming video, send e-mail, and spend hours visiting Web sites for pure entertainment purposes. With the click of a mouse, businesses can now leap oceans and span the globe to connect with a potential vendor, supplier, or customer. By stretching the boundaries that once limited the reach of most businesses, the Internet has helped globalize modern commerce by bridging the geographical divide that once complicated global business activities. Such techonology now allows business to be conducted continents apart, twenty-four hours a day. Simply put, the Internet has evolved into an enormous commercial network that fosters electronic commerce and facilitates the real-time exchange of ideas, products, and services.

As Internet usage continues to grow, users point to the need for greater speed as the most important factor separating those who have an easy, comfortable experience with the Internet and those who experience problems accessing the Internet. People who access the Internet through dial-up modems, even 56-kbps dial-up modems, often complain about slow service. For dial-up users, even the connection process can be a frustrating experience. Such users complain of being annoyed by the noise of a dial-up modem negotiating a connection with the Internet Service Provider (ISP), failed connection attempts, and slow service once the connection is made, especially when downloading graphics or sending and receiving large e-mail attachments.

As businesses increasingly rely on communications-related applications, acquiring and distributing timely and accurate information becomes critical to retaining a competitive edge in today's high-pressure business environment. High-speed Internet access, therefore, saves businesses more than just time; it translates into real-dollar savings with reduced time spent, increased productivity, and quicker response times overall. A faster connection to the resources available on the Internet means that a user is not waiting on a slow connection and wasting money or opportunity cost. More importantly, a faster connection enables faster transmission of information to the market or the end user. In addition to faster access to the Internet and increased bandwidth, broadband connections promise another equally attractive feature for end users: broadband connections to the Internet are "always on" so a user does not have to dial in to establish a connection. This added convenience means that users are more likely to use the Internet to research, exchange information, engage in electronic commerce, respond to vendors, suppliers, or customers, or otherwise enhance their business activities.

The solution to the heightened user demand for greater speed and "always-on" features is to increase the overall amount of capacity (i.e. bandwidth) of the network transmission lines through which voice, data and/or video flows. Bandwidth is a measure of the amount of data a transmission medium can carry and is often used interchangeably with capacity, also a measure of the amount of data a transmission medium can carry. The greater the bandwidth, the greater the capacity. However, the greater the bandwidth, the greater the cost.

Bandwidth also refers to a transmission medium's capacity to transmit data in bits per second.[1] Traditionally, communication channels were called bands. Technologists refer to the existing voice networks, which transmit information at rates below 56 Kbps (kilo bits per second),[2] as narrowband. Anything faster than 56 Kbps, but slower than 1.5 Mbps (mega bits per second),[3] is referred to as wideband, and anything faster than 1.5 Mbps is referred to as broadband.

The Last Mile Defined

By broadening the bandwidth of telecommunications transmission media, it is possible to construct broadband networks that deliver high-speed access to the Internet. While the technological requirements involved in such measures are manageable at this point of technological evolution, the inherent cost is anything but manageable. Broadband communications depend upon costly infrastructure investment because it may require the combination of various modems, transmission lines, and networking systems. Over the years, the telecommunications industry has invested billions of dollars in either upgrading the legacy copper wire infrastructure installed by Ma Bell and the other phone companies or installing new transmission media, such as fiber optics, to establish a nationwide broadband transport network. Even with millions of miles of broadband transport network linking cities to cities, broadband telecommunications services are not ubiquitous because most of the subscriber networks connecting homes and office buildings to the broadband transport networks do not have broadband transmission capabilities. As a result, many small and medium-sized businesses clustered in multi-tenanted office buildings have not reaped the benefits of the recent bandwidth explosion because their buildings do not have a broadband infrastructure in place which would allow high-speed access.

---

1. A bit is the contraction of the words "binary digits," and is the smallest unit of data retrievable through the yes/no digital signals stored in a computer's memory. Bps is an acronym for bits per second. See Harry Newton, *Newton's Telecom Dictionary*, Sixteenth Edition, Expanded and Updated, February 2000.
2. Kbps is an acronym for kilobits per second, i.e., thousands of bits per second, used to describe the speed of a network connection. Today's fastest modem operates at 56 kbps over an analog telephone line.
3. Mbps is an acronym for megabits per second, i.e., millions of bits per second, used to describe the speed of a network connection. Many local area networks operate at speeds of 10 mbps or more.

Unlike large businesses, which have the resources and requirements to lease dedicated, high-speed T-1 or T-3 lines[4] from the telephone company, small and medium-sized businesses cannot afford to implement their own broadband solutions to access the Internet. In most office buildings, small and medium-sized businesses use slow, dial-up modems and twisted-pair copper wire infrastructure to connect computers to the Information Super-highway.[5] The gap between these office buildings and the nearest "on ramp" to the high-speed networks is referred to as the "last mile." To better visual-ize the difference between using the century-old, dial-up, twisted-pair copper wire infrastructure and the new high-speed broadband transport network, imagine using a common garden hose and then switching to a high-pressured fire hose.

With rapid evolution of computing technology and technological ad-vancements in memory and processing devices, computers are now equipped with networking capabilities, increased processing speeds, and almost limit-less storage capabilities. The dial-up connections are no match for the giga-bit per second processing speeds of today's computers and multi-gigabits per second transmission rates of fiber-optic broadband networks. For this reason, a considerable amount of money has been and will continue to be invested in technological innovations and telecommunications service offerings that promise to close the last mile gap by broadening the bandwidth of the sub-scriber network.

Closing the Last Mile Gap

Capitalizing on the exploding demand for broadband services, a new breed of maverick telecommunications startup companies emerged in 1998, each hoping to close the last mile gap. These companies, known in the industry as building local exchange carriers (BLECs), raced to partner with building owners to provide widely affordable and flexible customized high-speed communications services to last mile building tenants. They competed with each other fiercely to offer innovative voice and data services featuring "al-ways-on" connection at speeds many times faster than the standard dial-up

---

4. A T-1 line is a high speed, high capacity network link used on the Internet. A T-1 line wide-area-network connection operates at 1.544 mega bits per second. A T-1 line carries 24 voice channels over copper wire, and the T-3 system, which can transport 28 T-1 signals (equivalent to supporting 672 voice calls), is used by users who need greater capacity than the T-1 offerings. Chapter 2 will provide a more detailed overview of these services.
5. Information Superhighway is a phrase coined by former Vice President Al Gore to describe all of the new ways to communicate electronically.

service. Tired of the lead-footed bureaucracy, high prices, and inflexible service plans of the giant telecommunications companies, small and medium-sized businesses embraced these BLECs. For example, these entrepreneurial startups offered "burstable bandwidth service plans," allowing customers to increase bandwidth temporarily in response to heavy data traffic while still paying a rate based on their average data traffic. Further technological innovations, a competition-friendly regulatory environment, and the raging bull market of the late 1990s led to the creation of hundreds of these BLECs, all eager to satisfy the insatiable demand for affordable high-speed telecommunications services among small and medium-sized businesses.

Anxious to please Wall Street and hoping to reap enormous riches, these BLECs rushed to sign as many building access agreements as possible, far outpacing their ability to provide the promised services to the building tenants. Building owners, eager to cultivate the financial potential in previously unused and unprofitable spaces, created new types of facilities to meet the specialized needs of commercial tenants who relied heavily on technology and telecommunications. Investor euphoria of the late 1990s encouraged risk-friendly investment bankers to continue to pour billions into the U.S. telecommunications sector, leading to fierce competition and overinvestment in broadband technologies. Adopting a "build it and they will come" credo, the BLECs rushed to deploy expensive broadband infrastructure in multi-tenant buildings. However, the customers and the demand for high-speed last mile communications services never met expectations.

The bull market's stampede slowed down to a veritable graze in the year 2000, crushing the stock prices of the once high-flying telecommunications companies infamous for their nosebleed valuations. The crash in stock prices came just as the BLECs were in their greatest need of capital to continue funding their network buildout. None of these BLECs were profitable and suddenly tech-averse investment bankers shut off the cash flow, even for high-yield debt financing. By depriving the telecommunications sector of the funding it depended on to construct its new-age broadband networks, Wall Street triggered a wave of bankruptcies in the telecommunications industry rivaling the merger-mania of the late 1990s. The mind-numbing potential of the miracle economy of the late 1990s started to look less miraculous each day as even the highest-flying companies spiraled headlong into a wave of bankruptcies and consolidations. The telecommunications sector, once crowded with entrepreneurial startups, is now dominated by giant companies and a handful of competitive startups. Struggling to survive and hoping to avoid becoming bait for bottom feeders, the remaining BLECs and giant telecommunications companies are hoarding cash and focusing on milking revenue from their existing networks. For reasons that extend beyond the collapse of the telecommunications sector, most telecommunications companies are canceling projects and selling assets to reduce leverage and increase liquidity.

The combination of high profile corporate scandals, bankruptcies, the September 11, 2001 tragedy, and the collapse of the telecommunications sector in general, accentuated by the Worldcom, Enron, Winstar, Teligent and Adelphia bankruptcies, has created a dramatic change in the perception of risk among investors, lenders and rating agencies. Wary of the telecommunications sector in general, lenders and institutional investors have increased their scrutiny of balance-sheet and off-balance-sheet transactions of target telecommunications companies. Lenders and institutional investors are now engaging in a deeper analysis of how companies will generate recurring cash flow to support their future network build-out plans.

Moreover, in light of the much-publicized accounting scandals of 2002 in general, and the suspected earnings manipulation by companies like Global Crossing in particular, investors and lenders view corporate accounting books and projected earnings with skepticism and perceive such reports of telecommunications companies to be less predictable and sustainable than in the past. As a result, investors and lenders are now discounting the growth prospects of new entrepreneurial startups and are instead focusing on liquidity and leverage in light of the perceived higher risk. This higher level of scrutiny, unfortunately, does not bode well for the business models of most telecommunications startups that depend on excessive infrastructure investment in the short term, with hopes of future returns if the infrastructure is fully built and utilized by potential customers.

Real estate owners have also adjusted their attitudes towards BLECs and other telecommunications companies. Even though demand for broadband communications continues to be robust among building tenants, building owners and managers are approaching all telecommunications companies with increased caution because they may have been stung by the collapse of their broadband vendors. Building owners are now scrutinizing BLECs and other emerging growth companies with particular care and, when possible, are attempting to structure new broadband deals mainly with large companies that have proven staying power. More importantly, in evaluating the credit profiles of the broadband vendors, building owners have intensified the bottom-up scrutiny of how a potential broadband vendor plans to generate recurring free cash flow and what might affect such cash flow over time.

All is not lost, however. Pundits predict that the investment bubble of the late 1990s and the now-predictable downswing of the business cycle will pave the way for major technological and economic advances as the telecommunications sector struggles to cleanse itself from the sins of the excesses of the late 1990s. A great deal has been written about the fast development and the even faster decline of the in-building broadband telecommunications sector, but we are not yet far enough away from the phenomenon to give proper weight to all of the lessons learned from the telecommunications debacle.

To conclude, demand for broadband communications among the underserved small and medium-sized businesses in commercial office buildings continues to be high. The actual number of telecommunications companies seeking to satisfy this demand has been reduced to a handful of struggling survivors, but the basic fundamentals supporting the telecommunications sector remain sensible. A combination of innovations in technology, regulatory incentives, well-structured, conservative business plans, and investor confidence in the overall market is necessary to breathe new life into the in-building broadband industry, which is desperately clinging to life support as the fatality rate among telecommunications companies continues to grow.

CHAPTER 2

A Technology Primer

Creation of the Multimedia Information Network

Modern telecommunication networks have evolved from a service specific information network that was designed to transport either voice, video, or data traffic to a multimedia information network that is capable of integrating all types of traffic into a single, high performance, bandwidth-intensive transport network. In the United States, regulatory and legal constraints forced separation of telecommunications services. For example, due to regulatory constraints, telephone companies were not allowed to provide cable television services in the same servicing area and vice versa. Telephone companies were forbidden to provide even advanced data services unless such services were offered through a subsidiary of the parent telephone company. A consequence of this forced separation of telecommunications industries was the deployment of telecommunications transport networks that were designed to handle service specific information. Thus, the century-old copper infrastructure installed by the phone companies was well equipped to handle voice traffic, but not data or video signals. This fact posed few problems for almost a century because, until recently, the telephone company's copper wires carried mostly voice traffic.

Once regulatory barriers were lifted and competition was encouraged, telephone companies upgraded their existing infrastructure to support transmission of multimedia services. Hoping to meet the explosive demand for multimedia telecommunications services, telephone companies, cable television companies, low earth orbit satellite companies, and even utility companies dove head-first into the development of new technologies and transmission media that could handle bandwidth-intensive multimedia telecommunications services. The later chapters will treat the various broadband access transmission technologies that allow telephone and cable companies to use their existing infrastructure to provide high-speed, broadband services.

These chapters will also deal with newer transmission technologies, such as fiber optics, that are designed specifically for the new age multimedia services. Before we deal with transmission technologies, however, it is important to understand basic technology concepts. In this Chapter, therefore, we will briefly describe analog and digital transmission schemes.

Overview of the Analog Network

Soon after the invention of the telephone in 1876, a public telephone network was designed to transmit speech and carry voice traffic. From the beginning and until the late 1960s, much of this public telephone network was analog, which meant that telephone calls were transmitted as analog signals that traveled through copper wires as electromagnetic waves. In this context, the term signal represents information in the form of voice, video, or data. Signals do not always convey the required information directly or free from disturbances, unless processed in some fashion. By converting signals to electrical form for processing, the early telephone networks were capable of enhancing, extracting, storing, and transmitting useful information in a commercially viable manner.

In telephone transmission, the term "analog" is used to suggest that the signal being transmitted is "analogous" to the original signal. In other words, in analog transmission schemes, voice and visual information are transmitted through communications pathways in the form of signals that exactly reproduce the sound or image being transmitted. An analog signal, if described by a mathematical expression or graphically by a curve or set of tabulated values, can be illustrated as continuous functions, usually of time and frequency. For example, consider a frequency-domain representation of a sound wave depicted in the form of a sinusoid, the familiar form of which is the oscillating periodic time waveform. In an analog transmission, each sinusoid wave, when transmitted, is reflected as a signal which is analogous or similar to the original signal. The speed of these analog signals is expressed in frequency, which refers to the number of times per second that a wave oscillates or swings back and forth in a complete cycle from the lowest point to the highest point. A complete cycle is measured by first recording the zero point of voltage, which is the starting point of the sine wave. From this starting point, the wave oscillates to the highest positive part of the wave, then swings back to the lowest negative part of the wave and then finally returns to the zero starting point of voltage, thus completing the cycle. The number of times per second that the wave completes this cycle by traveling from the starting point to its end point constitutes the frequency of the analog signal. The higher the speed or frequency, the more complete cycles of a wave are completed in a period of time. The speed or frequency of a sine wave is measured in hertz (Hz) or cycles per second. One hertz equals one complete cycle per second so, for example, a wave that oscillates or swings back and forth to complete one hundred cycles per second has a speed or frequency of one hundred hertz. Abbreviated forms are used to express speeds for analog services. For example, thousands of cycles per second are expressed as kilohertz (KHz) and millions of cycles per second are expressed as megahertz (MHz).

It is helpful to understand the mechanics of sound in order to understand the workings of an analog network. The term sound typically refers to the successive compression and refraction of air, although sound is also used to include solid and liquid vibrations. For example, when a person speaks, the vibrations in the vocal chord generate sound waves which compress the air in cycles. These vibrations occur in the direction of the wave motion, traveling to the listener's ear by compressing the air between the speaker and the listener. When the pressure variations reach the listener's ear, the compressed air is converted to nerve impulses which are then sent to the auditory center of the brain for decoding into useful information. In a telephone voice call, the sound generated in a person's vocal chord creates fluctuations in air pressure and the resulting sound waves travel to, and strike, the diaphragm located within the telephone handset. When the sound waves strike the diaphragm, the diaphragm vibrates and an electrical circuit within the telephone handset opens and closes, converting the vibrations into electrical current with approximately the same frequencies as the original sound waves. A device called the transmitter, which is located within a telephone handset, converts the speaker's sound or acoustical energy into electrical energy which represent the sounds of the speaker's voice. Because this electrical current is similar to the original sound waves, the resulting signal which is transmitted in the form of electrical current in the telephone handset is referred to as an analog signal.

Analog transmissions, as well as digital transmissions, take place in either guided or unguided media. Examples of guided media include coaxial cable, cable TV and copper wires used for telephone services. Unguided media examples include microwave, home wireless telephones and cellular car phones. Analog signals, such as voice, radio and TV signals, travel within a specified range of frequency bands within the respective medium. The speed at which the information travels within the frequency band is measured by subtracting the lower range of the frequency band from the higher range. For example, in telephone transmission, voice travels between the range of 300 to 3400 hertz or cycles per second and, as a result, the speed that voice travels within the public network equals 3100 hertz or cycles per second, which is 3400 Hz minus 300 Hz. The voice frequency range of 300 Hz to

3400 Hz is known as the voice band of frequencies. Any frequency below 300 Hz is filtered out to remove electrical interference and other noise induced from adjacent power lines or electrical wires. Like the lower frequencies, any frequency above 3400 Hz is also filtered out and, as a result, the actual bandwidth of the filtered signal is measured at 3100 Hz.

An analog signal, like sound, is susceptible to various obstacles as it travels within the transmission path. As it travels, sound loses its intensity because of reduction of signal strength over distance and is subject to interference because of collisions of waveforms with other sources of energy. Similarly, an analog signal weakens as it travels over distances whether it is sent over guided or unguided media. Typically, the signal meets resistance or interference in the transmission medium over which it is sent, which causes the signal to fade or weaken. In voice conversation, for example, a voice may sound softer as it travels over distances. In addition to becoming weaker, an analog signal may pick up electrical interference, or "noise" on the line, and, as a result, can transmit static or crud, along with the transmitted signal. The sources for such electrical interference or "noise" are limitless and include adjacent power lines, lights and electric machinery, all of which create noise in the form of electrical energy. The occasional static heard during voice conversations in analog lines is a result of such electrical interference.

In an analog network, a device called an amplifier is used to overcome resistance within transmission media and to periodically boost the signal strength of the analog wave. The amplifier is not a perfect solution, however. Although the amplifier boosts the signal strength of the analog wave being transmitted, it is not able to separate the electrical interference present in the form of noise from the actual transmitted voice or data. As a result, both the noise as well as the transmitted signal is amplified, which creates the static or unintelligible noise that is heard in some voice telephone calls transmitted through analog lines.

Notwithstanding the presence of such static or electrical interference, most people can still understand a static-filled telephone conversation for the most part. In a data transmission, on the other hand, computers are not capable of separating the data being transmitted from noise or electrical interference. As a consequence, when noise or electrical interference is amplified on data transmissions, serious errors can be created in the transmission process. For example, in a real estate agreement of sale, the purchase price amount of $1 million can be transmitted in error as $100 million due to electrical interference. The computer, unfortunately, will not recognize such error in transmission. In contrast to analog transmissions, digital transmission schemes regenerate the original information and, as a result, do not amplify unnecessary noise or electrical interference. In digital transmissions, devices called repeaters recover the digital data being transmitted, recreate an exact bit-for-bit copy of the original information, and retransmit the digital data, without the extraneous noise or electrical interference, at full strength towards the end destination. For this and many other reasons, the telephone networks have migrated from analog to digital transmissions.

Migrating from Analog to Digital Transmission: The Digital Revolution

Older, analog services were not equipped to handle the bandwidth-intensive applications services that came into demand in the later years and, when Internet usage and call volumes increased, it became necessary to switch to digital telephone lines. Digital signals have certain advantages over analog waves in that the signals are faster, can accommodate more capacity, and contain fewer transmission errors. As a result, today's high-speed networks carry mostly digital signals.

Digital transmission schemes use a binary code to represent information and, as a result, the transmitted information is converted into a string of 0s and 1s. The signal capacity characteristic associated with digital signals is called a bit rate, which is the number of bits a communications channel can support. The term "bit" is a contraction of the words "binary digits." For example, consider a comparison of a transmission medium that transports data at the rate of 1 megabit per second (1 mbps or one million binary digits per second), and a transmission medium that transports data at the rate of 1 kilobit per second (1 kbps or one thousand binary digits per second). Both facilities deliver the same quantity of information, but the 1 megabit per second transmission facility delivers the information in only 1/1000 of the time as the 1 kilobit per second transmission facility.

As with analog networks, digital signals lose strength as they travel over longer distances, and therefore, the signals are amplified at various intervals within the network. In digital transmission, regenerative repeaters throughout the digital network recreate the original signal. During this regeneration process, electrical interference and noise are filtered out from the transmitted information. The reconstructed digital information is then sent through the network sequentially so that it can travel longer distances, but unlike analog transmissions, the newly reconstructed digital information does not carry any noise or electrical interference. Digital signals travel as discrete breaks or a series of on and off blips. In contrast, an analog signal travels as continuous waves.

An analog signal is converted to a digital signal by a coding system called Pulse Code Modulation (PCM). During the PCM process, information above or below the frequency range of 300 Hz to 3400 Hz is first filtered out. Then the analog signal is sampled at the rate of 8000 times per second. The output of this sampling process is known as a Pulse Amplitude Modulated (PAM) signal. The amplitude of the PAM signal is then measured and assigned a value between 0 and +127 to define its amplitude. Finally, the value of each sample is encoded into a series of electrical pulses or a stream of 8 bit-code. A string of 8 bits make up a byte.

The PCM process, described above, requires a 64,000 bits per second channel to sample a voice call 8000 times per second. Thus, in the PCM process, 8000 samples are transmitted per second and, with a sample size of 8 bits, the resulting data rate is 64,000 bits per second. In other words, 8000 samples multiplied by the 8 bit-code equals 64,000 bits per second. This is known as Digital Signal Level Zero (DS-0). DS-0 is the basic building block of the digital network, and has sufficient capacity for a one-voice telephone call. By stacking together 24 DS-0 channels, plus signaling information, the DS-0 signals are bundled into DS-1 which is the next level in the digital hierarchy. Thus, 24 channels multiplied by 64,000 bits per second, plus some signaling information, equals 1.544 million bits per second.

The creation of the digital hierarchy is made possible by a process known as multiplexing. The process of multiplexing enables multiple devices to share the same transmission path, thus, increasing the amount of information that can be transmitted over the same media, without the need for constructing new transmission media. By combining and then transmitting two or more individual signals over the same transmission path, multiplexing schemes create more capacity within the same transmission medium. In digital networks, a technique called time division multiplexing (TDM) is used to combine several digital signals onto a single transmission path. For example, 24 channels are time division multiplexed together to form the DS-1 level of the digital hierarchy.

Analog networks first used a multiplexing technique called frequency division multiplexing (FDM) to transmit analog telephone calls through trunk lines that ran between telephone company's switching offices. In FDM, the total bandwidth of the transmission line is divided into separate frequency bands, which are capable of carrying a separate signal. Information is then transmitted continuously in its very own assigned frequency band. The different frequency bands, once stacked together, form the various subchannels that occupy the total frequency bandwidth of the transmission path. For example, early multiplexing schemes constructed the T-1 line, which provides 24 channels on the same telephone line, and, since the creation of the T-1 line, newer multiplexing schemes have created more advanced medium such as a T-3 line, which provides 672 channels on the same telephone line.

In addition to multiplexing schemes, a technique known as compression is used to add capacity within a transmission medium. Compression squeezes large amounts of data into smaller sizes, thus, enabling the transmission of bandwidth-intensive applications such as graphics, x-ray images, and video. It is important to note that compression does not alter the information being transmitted, but merely reduces the bandwidth or number of bits needed to represent or encode the information. By compressing the information, it is possible to add capacity within transmission lines, save transmission time, and add storage space within storage devices such as hard disks.

CHAPTER 3

Overview

Services

Despite the downturn in the economy, which led to the fall of many upstart telecommunications companies, the surviving telecommunications service providers continue to roll out facilities-based, bundled local and long distance phone service, high-speed Internet, and other broadband-related services to multi-tenanted commercial office buildings in which small and medium-sized businesses are clustered. These telecommunications companies have invested and will continue to invest substantial amounts of infrastructure and marketing expenses in these buildings, with the hopes that they will generate sufficient revenues from building tenants to fund their operating expenses. For the telecommunications company, successful penetration of a dense office building could mean that it is able to (i) increase the number of customers it serves in the local market, (ii) increase the potential revenues per customer it can generate by cross-marketing bundled services, (iii) lower the costs of adding new customers to the network, and (iv) reduce the costs of providing services by capturing economies of scale.

In order to sell and market these broadband services to the building's tenants, the telecommunications company typically has to negotiate a telecommunications access agreement with the building owner. The access agreements allow service providers to access the building's risers, conduits, existing riser cable and inside wiring, and other building space in the telephone or mechanical equipment room to deliver broadband and related services to the building's tenants. By converting previously unutilized spaces and resources into potential revenue generators, these agreements have become a welcome source of unanticipated revenues for the building owner. In addition to serving as a source of profit for the building owner, the network build-out also serves as a free technology upgrade for the building. With the installation of a broadband infrastructure, the building owner has the ability to market broadband services as a leasing amenity to retain existing tenants and/or attract new tenants for the building.

This chapter and the subsequent chapters will highlight most, if not all, of the important issues typically raised during the preparation and negotiation of a telecommunications access agreement. The issues will be raised from both the building owner's and the telecommunications company's perspectives and, whenever possible, will provide the various possibilities for resolving the issues and drafting workable compromises. Without covering the subjects exhaustively, we will answer some of the important, broad questions that may arise in negotiating these issues. Hopefully the lessons the authors have learned from negotiating countless telecommunications agreements will serve as valuable guideposts for those who follow.

License, Lease, or Easement

The first and most obvious issue to consider and define is the nature and scope of the relationship between the parties to the telecommunications access agreement. An access agreement between a building owner and a telecommunications company can be structured as (i) a license agreement, (ii) an easement agreement, or (iii) a lease agreement. Obviously, a telecommunications company will want the broadest rights possible and will attempt to avail itself of typical rights afforded to holders of easements or tenancy interests. From the building owner's perspective, however, the access agreement should be structured as a grant of a non-exclusive license and not as an easement, lease, or other interest in property. A sample provision providing that the access agreement is only a license, and not an easement or a lease agreement, states the following:

> This Agreement creates a license only and Licensee acknowledges that Licensee does not have and shall not claim at any time any interest or estate of any kind or extent whatsoever in the Building or Premises by virtue of this Agreement or Licensee's use of the Premises pursuant hereto. In connection with the foregoing, Licensee further acknowledges that in no event shall the relationship between Licensor and Licensee be deemed to be a so-called landlord-tenant relationship and that in no event shall Licensee be entitled to avail itself of any rights afforded to tenants under the laws of the state in which the Building is located. This Agreement is not and does not grant an easement.

As an added precaution, a building owner should include language restricting the telecommunications company from recording the agreement or any memorandum in the public real estate records of the jurisdiction in which the building is located.

Notwithstanding these attempts by the building owner to structure the access agreement as a license, it is likely that a court seeking to enforce the agreement will interpret the agreement as an unrecorded lease, not a license. This is because, despite the fact that the agreement is called a license, a typical access agreement mirrors a lease agreement in that it contains sufficiently detailed provisions relating to term, renewal options, defaults and remedies, and termination rights. Prevailing custom in the telecommunications industry, however, is to label these agreements as licenses even though practitioners generally recognize that the agreements will be enforced as a lease.

Defining Services

It is difficult, if not impossible, to predict the next technological evolution or innovation in the broadband space and the manner in which the marketplace will treat the business arrangement between building owners and service providers with respect to such a new technology offering. From the building owner's perspective, therefore, the challenge is to transact in a sufficiently intelligent manner so as to preserve flexibility and adaptability to both the ever-changing technology of the industry and the constantly evolving demands of the business community. The access agreement should preserve the building owner's ability to generate future income if a new technology offering is introduced in the building for which the marketplace dictates profit sharing between building owners and service providers. From a drafting standpoint, then, the agreement should enumerate the various technology offerings that the service provider will deliver to building tenants on the effective date of the agreement, with the understanding that the parties will negotiate in good faith additional licensee fees for new technology offerings that are not listed as a "Permitted Service" in an agreement.

Typically, a telecommunications company seeking to provide broadband services generally delivers high-speed Internet access and other Internet-related communications services. While most industry experts would agree that Internet-related communications services include such services as voice, video, data, and facsimile, other unintended technology offerings could become part of the overall deal if the building owner fails to exclude specific services from the definition of permitted services. From a telecommunications company's standpoint, a comprehensive definition of permitted services which enumerates the specific technology offerings that it intends to sell in the building might avoid unnecessary disputes with the landlord during the term of the agreement. A sample definition of communication services reads:

"Communication Services" or "Services" shall mean high-speed Internet access and other Internet-related communication services that Licensee may provide within a Building to Tenants of such Building subject to the terms of this Agreement, and may include all other services such as voice, video, data, facsimile or other communication services (or any combination of the foregoing) that Licensee may provide within a Building to Tenants of such Building subject to the terms of this Agreement. These Services may include, without limitation, (i) the provision and re-sale of local exchange services and point-to-point telephone communications (including dedicated long-distance service); (ii) video communications service; (iii) 800 or other toll-free-number service; (iv) telephone credit or debit card service; (v) audio conferencing, paging, voice mail and message center service; (vi) data transmission service; (vii) access to computer "Internet" or other networked computer-based communications and related content, including access via Internet "portal" service; (viii) provision of telephone, video communication or other communications equipment or infrastructure to the users of such Services in connection with their use of such Services; and (ix) any consulting or like telecommunications or Internet-related professional services.

In the context of a telecommunications access agreement, the building owner and the telecommunications service provider have a symbiotic relationship in that both serve the building's tenants. As a provider of broadband services to the building's tenants, the telecommunications company is neither a space tenant nor the building owner's service provider. The building owner merely allows the service provider to access the building in order to create a leasing amenity for the building's tenants. Because the telecommunications company, not the building owner, provides the telecommunications services to the building occupants, it is important to clarify in the Agreement the respective roles of each party to ensure that neither party becomes responsible for unexpected obligations.

Default Scenarios

A 20-30 day notification period should be set that allows each party to terminate the agreement under certain circumstances if the situation cannot be remedied.

Non-Payment

The building owner can terminate the agreement if the vendor fails to pay required fees.

Failure to Fulfill Obligations of Agreement

The building owner can terminate the agreement if the vendor fails to fulfill the obligations specified in the access agreement and cannot or does not remedy the situation.

Bankruptcy of the Vendor

The building owner can terminate the agreement if the vendor files for bankruptcy or commences any other proceeding or case under the Federal Bankruptcy Code or under any similar federal or state statute.

Casualty Damage

If any part of the building is damaged by fire or other casualty, the vendor should give prompt written notice to Licensor. If the damage is so extensive that substantial alteration or reconstruction would be required or in any other event that the building owner determines that it is not economical or otherwise desirable to repair the damage, the building owner should have the right to terminate the agreement.

If the owner does not elect to terminate the agreement, the owner should restore the areas used by the vendor to the same condition in which they existed before sustaining the damage. If the owner does not do this or the building becomes unsuitable for use by the vendor, each party should be allowed to terminate the agreement.

Condemnation and Eminent Domain

If the building should be taken for any public or quasi-public use, by right or eminent domain or otherwise or should be sold in lieu of condemnation, then the agreement should terminate as of the date when physical possession of the building is taken by the condemning authority.

Termination of Agreement by Vendor

If the vendor has performed proper due diligence as part of the installation process, including a feasibility report (which should cover issues such as the feasibility of installing in the building, determining whether there are enough tenants to make service cost-effective, etc.), the vendor can use this as an exit strategy. Here are some examples of situations where the vendor can terminate the agreement:

- The building is not appropriate for the communications operations for economic or technological reasons.
- Interference with vendor's operations as a result of the use of any equipment operated at the building by the owner or any other party if the equipment is installed subsequent to the installation of the vendor's equipment.
- The building owner fails to fulfill the terms of the access agreement.
- The presence of hazardous or toxic materials not disclosed by the building owner.
- Any license, permit, or zoning variance required is not obtained, expires, or is withdrawn through no fault of the vendor.
- Situations in which the tenant mix changes, making continued service no longer feasible or cost effective.

Holding Over

If equipment remains in the building beyond the termination of the agreement without specific prior written approval from the building owner, the vendor should pay monthly license fees to the owner.

Milestone Schedule

A milestone schedule should be included with the access agreement. The schedule should include a description of the services to be provided by the vendor and should outline a time frame in which the services should be completed. The building owner should be required to have provided all information and materials that the vendor needs to complete the services according to this timeline. It is a good idea to specify a set period of time for the building owner to provide any information and materials required by the vendor to complete the services, such as 10 days following the vendor's request. If any delay occurs during this time period, the period the vendor has to complete the services can be extended to reflect the delay.

Any specifications related to any products or deliverables related to the services should be included. The building owner should be given the right to inspect and test each product and deliverable produced by the vendor to determine if conformance to the specifications has been met. If the building owner discovers any defect or is unsatisfied with any deliverable, the owner should be required to provide a written notice stating the defect in reasonable detail within the time frame specified. There should be a period of time specified, such as 30 days, during which the vendor has the opportunity to remedy the situation and correct any defects. The submission and review process will then be repeated until each product and deliverable conforms to the specifications. However, during this process, the milestone schedule must not be breached, and the vendor must be exercising due diligence to address and correct any deficiencies and defects.

Quality of Services

Performance Standards

Equally, if not more, important than delineating the precise scope and definition of the types of permitted services that the telecommunications service providers are able to deliver in the building is imposing performance guidelines on service providers to ensure the proper scope and quality of the telecommunications services. In an ever-competitive leasing market, ensuring that a building offers the latest telecommunications amenities that are available to tenants of other buildings in the area is crucial. In order to capture a competitive edge, the access agreement should impose certain performance requirements on the telecommunications company. For starters, the agreement should ensure that the building's telecommunications service providers are offering the most modern, competitive and effective broadband services to building tenants at the most competitive prices. Moreover, the agreement should require service providers to deliver to the building's tenants all services that are available to their other customers within the metropolitan area in which the building is located. Lastly, the agreement should require the service provider to upgrade its broadband networks periodically to meet the highest quality standards of the telecommunications industry. Because the market's appetite for bandwidth might increase during the term of the access agreement, the agreement should require service providers to maintain access speeds at all times that are competitive with the market for Internet services. Of course, what is considered state-of-the-art in a particular area or region of the county might be different elsewhere.

Sample provisions setting forth these performance guidelines state:

> Licensee shall, at all times during the term hereof, use commercially reasonable efforts to meet the highest quality standards of the industry while providing the Services to the Tenants at a commercially reasonable and competitive price. During the term hereof, Licensee shall at its own cost, operate, maintain, repair, replace and periodically upgrade the Telecommunications Facilities. Further, Licensee shall make commercially reasonable, good faith efforts to maintain modern and effective high-speed Internet connections and other improvements related to the scope, nature and quality of the Services as technology is improved, and to maintain access speeds which are competitive with the market for Internet services.

Licensor may from time to time request that Licensee provide in the Building one or more telecommunications services not then currently being offered by Licensee to Tenants of such Building but that are then being offered by other telecommunications providers in the metropolitan area in which the Building is located (or being marketed for introduction in such metropolitan area). If Licensee does not, within thirty (30) days after receipt of a written request from Licensor, agree to provide such non-offered services in the Building on a timetable and basis reasonably acceptable to Licensor, then Licensor shall have the right, at its option, to contract for such additional services from another telecommunications provider. Licensee shall have the right to charge Tenants a competitive price or fee for any such additional services.

Requiring Telecom Companies to Address Service Problems

In addition to defining the respective rights and responsibilities of the parties, the Agreement should provide for a Tenant complaint system which ensures that the telecommunications company, not the building owner, will be responsible for service interruption and responsive to quality control complaints. The complaint processing system should include a contact telephone number, a processing and logging system to track system problems, and the company's response times and the resolution of all complaints. In addition to clarifying the building owner's lack of responsibility with respect to the quality or sufficiency of services to building Tenants, the building owner should also limit the scope of its responsibilities as they pertain to the telecommunications company. A sample provision establishing a clear understanding between the parties regarding respective responsibilities pertaining to building tenants states:

Licensee shall be solely responsible for billing and collections for the Licensee's Services. Licensee shall be solely responsible for performing its own evaluations of the financial responsibility, creditworthiness and character of each Tenant. Licensee agrees that Licensor has expressly disclaimed any knowledge or warranty with respect to the financial condition of any Tenant and that Licensee is proceeding at its own risk in entering into subscription agreements with Tenants and performing Services for Tenants. Licensor shall have no responsibility for, or obligation or liability with respect to, (i) the quality, suitability, reliability or operation of the Telecommunications Equipment or Services, (ii) compliance with applicable laws and regulations with respect thereto, or (iii) the compatibility of the Licensee's equipment with the heating, ventilation, air conditioning, plumbing, electrical, fire protection, safety, security, public utility, or other systems at the Building. Licensee does not rely on the fact, nor does Licensor represent, that any specific Tenant or type or number of Tenants shall, during the term of this Agreement, or any renewals or extensions thereof, occupy space in the Building.

Electromagnetic Interference

A carrier's telecommunications equipment could generate electrical and electromagnetic outputs, radio frequency and other electromagnetic signals or noise which could interfere with the building systems, elevators and other telecommunications equipment located in the building. Similarly, signal leakage and other electromagnetic and electrical outputs from the building's systems and equipment could interfere with the smooth operation of the carrier's in-building broadband infrastructure. Such interference could expose both the telecommunications company and the building owner to potential liabilities if service failure resulting from such interference causes actual or consequential damages. From the building owner's perspective, the agreement should require that the telecommunications equipment installed by the telecom carrier will not interfere electrically or in any other manner with the equipment or other operations of the building owner or the other tenants or licensees in the building. The agreement should also address procedures for requiring the telecom carrier to remedy the situation if such interference interrupts other equipment in the building.

The carrier's counsel should require similar protection from the building owner by requiring the building owner to intervene if other equipment in the building interferes electrically or otherwise with the carrier's equipment. A sample interference provision reads:

Neither the Owner nor anyone operating on its behalf will tap or otherwise interfere with the System for any purposes. Notwithstanding anything else in this Agreement to the contrary, the Company shall not interfere with the right of an individual resident to install or use his own private reception device, provided, however, that should any device or any facility belonging to a resident (or Owner) not comply with the technical specifications established by the FCC, including, but not limited to, signal leakage, which interferes with the Company's delivery of the Services, the Company reserves the right to discontinue service to the Premises, or, at the Company's discretion, the individual unit, until such non-conformance is cured by the Owner or resident as the case may be. If, at any time during the Term, (i) any electrical output, electromagnetic output, radio frequency, or other electromagnetic signals or noise resulting from the operation of the System, in the reasonable opinion of Owner, adversely affects the equipment, machinery, or systems of Owner or residents, or causes degradation of reception or transmission on the equipment of other telecommunications service providers in the Premises (collectively, "Interference"), and (ii) Company does not correct the Interference within twenty-four (24) hours after receipt of telephonic or written notice from Owner, Company will immediately cease operations (except for intermittent testing on a schedule approved by Owner) until the Interference has been corrected to the satisfaction of Owner. If such Interference has not been corrected within thirty (30) days after receipt of Owner's notice, Owner will, in addition to any other remedies available to Owner, have the right to immediately terminate this Agreement by written notice. If, in the reasonable opinion of Owner, Interference is creating imminent danger of injury to person or property ("Emergency"), Owner will give verbal notice (either in person or by telephone) of the Emergency to Company, who will act immediately to remedy the Emergency, and Owner will have the right to shut down the System immediately until the Emergency is resolved. Company shall Indemnify and Defend the Owner Parties against, and Waives all Claims against the Owner Parties arising, or alleged to arise, out of any Interference or shutdown of the System in accordance with the provisions of this paragraph.

Installing a Cable Distribution System

This concept is very important from the owner's point of view. The building owner should reserve the right to install and operate a central telecommunications Cable Distribution System (CDS) in the building. The agreement should specify the following:

- The CDS may include a main cross-connect (MC) for use by competitive service providers to reach tenant demarcation points in the Building.
- The MC should be considered the demarcation point for service providers accessing the building and the origination point of the CDS.
- The telephone closet demarcation block on each floor of the building will serve as the termination point of the CDS on that floor.

- Once the building owner informs the vendor that the CDS is in place, the vendor will use the CDS to provide any new services to the customers that commence after the installation of the CDS. These new services and demarcation points should be connected to the CDS. The vendor will be responsible for any expenses incurred for this process.
- The building owner should reserve the right to charge all providers, including the vendor entering into an agreement with the owner, a fee for access to the CDS.
- The vendor should have the right to continue to use any equipment, cable, or conduit installed in the building that is being used to provide existing services to current customers before the CDS was installed. However, when the current specified term ends, the vendor will use the CDS for any new customers in the building.
- The building owner will be responsible for repairing or replacing the CDS only to the extent necessary to reach areas in the building used by Tenants. However, if the need for repairs or replacements was caused by the vendor, the vendor should be responsible for the cost.
- If the CDS malfunctions or is damaged or destroyed, the vendor is entitled to an equitable abatement of the annual license and CDS fees if it is related to the defect from the date the defect occurs until the date it is repaired. The vendor should also be given the right in such a situation to use the equipment and licensed areas to provide service to customers in the same manner as the vendor did before the installation of the new CDS.
- The building owner should provide the vendor with the contact information of the party responsible for the operation and maintenance of the CDS.
- The building owner should try to ensure that the vendor will not be able to make any claim for any damages whatsoever in connection with or arising from the CDS.
- The building owner should also reserve the right to assign or delegate its rights and obligations to another party. In such a situation, the building owner should obtain, in writing, an indemnification agreement on behalf of the vendor that holds the vendor harmless from and against any claims or liability arising from any malfunction, damage or destruction of the CDS, unless the vendor causes such an occurrence through negligence or willful misconduct.

Types of Technology Offerings

The rest of this chapter will provide an introduction to the various types of technology available to offer broadband service.

Modern Communications Networks and Switching Approaches

Defined in broad terms, a communications network is comprised of: (i) various pieces of equipment located at the subscriber's premises that are capable of receiving and transmitting information, (ii) transmission facilities that create the communications pathways through which information in the form of voice, data, or video flows from one location to another, and (iii) switching systems that interconnect the various transmission facilities at various locations to adjust traffic pathways of the information by linking various communications networks together. The larger communications systems are comprised of: (i) an interoffice network, which is a transmission line that links various telephone offices, and (ii) a subscriber network, which is a transmission line that links the subscriber to the telephone office. The transmission line within the interoffice network connecting the telephone offices is called the "Trunk," and the transmission line within the subscriber network connecting the subscriber to the telephone office is called the "Subscriber Loop" or the "Customer Loop."

Within these communications networks, information and control signals are transmitted from one location to another in either the analog or digital form and, as a result, any transmission can be described as either an analog transmission or digital transmission. In additionn, depending upon the transmission medium used to transport the information or signals, transmission can take the form of an electrical signal, optical transmission, or wireless (radio) transmission. The various high-speed Internet access technologies currently offered by most BLECs and large telecommunications companies are transported through four broad categories of transmission media: twisted-pair copper wires, optical fiber, coaxial cable, and fixed-wireless/microwave communications. These transmission facilities provide the communications path through which electric current, optical, or radio signals travel between points along the data transmission route. Cost and availability of each varies from market to market, and the later chapters briefly describe each technology.

A typical communications network transfers information between a source and a destination using connecting links that enable flow of signals among users. Establishing a direct and dedicated link between all of the random sources and the limitless destinations is practically impossible. For example, if you attempted to establish a direct wire line connection between your office telephone and every other user in the world, you would literally suffocate your office with wires, and even then you will not be able to establish a direct link with the rest of the world. One way to bypass the need to construct direct and dedicated connections between every user in the world is to develop a method that allows fewer transmission lines to connect a greater number of communications devices. "Switching" techniques do just that.

Switching Systems

Switches create interconnection between the various network transmission lines, between the lines and the trunks, or between the trunks. It is possible to visualize a switched network by using a roadway system to create an analogy. For the same reasons why establishing a direct transmission line between all of the users is not practical, it is not physically possible or cost efficient to build roads that establish a direct connection among all of the locations in a city. Our roadways stretch to limitless boundaries because of intersections that connect each road to a group of roads, which are similarly connected to other roads through additional intersections along the route. Switching stations are like highway intersections in that switches connect multiple transmission lines. Information traffic, like highway traffic, travels through a transmission line until it reaches a connecting switch. Once the information reaches a switching station, it is then routed to its desired destination through a connecting transmission line, which is similarly connected to other transmission lines within the switched network. The traffic, therefore, travels from the source point to the desired destination through switched communications networks.

A hierarchical network topology that connects clusters of users within defined geographical areas through an intertwined network of intermediate switching nodes enables transmission of data among many users in the most cost-effective and efficient manner. Advances in networking schemes have made it possible to efficiently and economically transmit signals from one physical point to another physical point, or several physical points, that stretch from local to international borders. Traditionally, communications networks have been classified into two topological categories: Wide Area Networks (WANs), and Local Area Networks (LANs). WANs consist of various interconnected nodes and transmission lines that cover large geographical areas with indefinite distances. Nodes represent switching facilities that link and route the flow of information or data from one node to the other until the information or data reaches the end point destination. LANs, on the other hand, connect communications devices over isolated networks within a small geographical space, typically a single building or a cluster of buildings.

Switches are placed in various locations within the national, regional and local networks to create interconnection between the various network transmission lines, between the lines and the trunks, or between the trunks. Multiplexers, which create more capacity within the same transmission medium by combining and then transmitting two or more individual signals over the same transmission path, are used to aggregate the traffic between longer distances in order to maximize efficiency. The multiplexed signals are concentrated into long distance transmission lines or "trunks." The trunks are interconnected by switches that transfer the signals from one trunk to the other. Once the signals reach a switching destination, a demultiplexer strips the aggregated signals and directs each signal to its appropriate destination. Routing technology determines the path of the signals across the network.

WANs utilize two different information transfer techniques to organize information for transmission, multiplexing, routing, and switching: circuit switching and packet switching. There are differences in the way these two switching systems transport information traffic from node to node and the paragraphs below describe each technology briefly. The later paragraphs also describe two related technologies that evolved from packet-switching techniques: frame relay and ATM.

Circuit-Switched Networks

The telephone network is the most common example of a circuit-switched network. A circuit-switched network establishes a dedicated, end-to-end connection between two stations through the nodes of the network. As a connection-oriented network, a circuit-switched network requires the setting up of a dedicated transmission path for the complete duration of the information transfer. As a result, before signals can be transmitted through the transmission lines, a dedicated circuit establishing a connection path which connects the caller and the call receiver must be established. The transmission link between the caller and the call receiver may not always be direct and, as a consequence, the various legs of the transmission might require internal switching of the signals within the network until the signals reach the desired destination. A typical circuit connection might require a transmission path that routes traffic through a number of switches and trunks. Therefore, an efficient and resilient routing strategy within the network architecture must be established before transmitting the signals through the network. In establishing such an efficient and resilient communications path, channel capacity of the transmission pathway is reserved in advance between the various switching stations or nodes and appropriate routing decisions are pre-determined to devise the most efficient and resilient transmission route for the signals.

This process, unfortunately, leads to waste of transmission capacity or bandwidth because a typical information transfer is not continuous. For example, in a typical voice call, there are moments of silence within the duration of the call where the transmission line is not utilized. In a circuit-switched network, the unutilized space and time are wasted because the circuit is reserved for the original call, and therefore, not available for transporting other signals during the duration of the original call. The circuit is reallocated for transfer of other calls or data only when the original call is terminated or released. Circuit-switching is even more inefficient with data transfer because most data transfers occur in bursts and with significant delays between each consecutive transfer.

In order to visualize the general steps involved in a circuit-switched network, consider how a typical telephone call transpires. Before a telephone call is placed, a dedicated circuit is first established for the transfer of voice traffic within the telephone network. The circuit-switching operation begins when the caller lifts the receiver off the hook. By picking up the receiver, the caller makes a call request with the local telephone office switching equipment. The call request is made in the form of an electrical current that is generated when the phone is lifted and which flows from the caller's phone to the local telephone office switching equipment. In response to the call request, the switching station prepares for the call and returns an audible dial tone signal back to the caller, indicating that the call request has been approved. The caller then dials the telephone number, which generates a sequence of pulses or tones that are translated by the switching equipment as a called address. The switching equipment then prepares to allocate the resources within the network to establish a dedicated transmission path within the switched network. The switch will create a transmission path that passes through a number of switches and trunks, if necessary, and, depending on traffic congestion or other transmission difficulties, will chart the route that is most cost efficient and resilient.

Once a dedicated, end-to-end transmission circuit is established, the destination local telephone office switch sends a ringing signal to the intended call recipient to alert that intended recipient of the incoming call. If the intended recipient is not busy, the destination local telephone office switch returns an audible ringing signal to the caller, which alerts the caller that a connection to the recipient will be made if the recipient is available to pick up the phone. If the intended call recipient is not available, the switch sends an audible busy signal to the caller, which alerts the caller that a dedicated end-to-end connection is not possible at that time. If the call recipient is not busy and if the phone is picked up, the switch terminates the ringing signal and initiates the message transfer phase of the call. A dedicated, end-to-end circuit connection is now reserved for the caller and the call recipient. The circuit connection is released only when the caller or the call recipient terminates the call by hanging up its respective phone.

In the foregoing example, the circuit-switched network establishes a dedicated end-to-end connection between the two callers. For the duration of the entire information transfer or voice call, the circuit remains occupied and, consequently, unavailable for the tranfer of other information until the circuit is released. Once the callers terminate the call, the circuit is then released and made available for other traffic. The routing decision for the information transfer, therefore, is pre-determined at the time the dedicated end-to-end connection is established. Once the circuit is identified, information travels through the interconnected transmission paths in the most efficient and cost-effective manner.

Packet-Switched Networks

A packet-switched network, like the circuit-switched network, is a collection of nodes interconnected by transmission links over indefinite distances. Unlike the circuit-switched network, a packet-switched network switches and transports signals in a cluster of bits that are switched and transmitted as a single unit or a "packet" across the network. By converting a user's data stream into small packets that can be routed through the network in bursts on a first-come, first-served basis, a packet-switched network wastes less bandwidth than a circuit-switched network. Packet-switching technology transports data signals more efficiently than a circuit-switched technology because, in packet-switching systems, connections between the networks are made only when the traffic is being transmitted, thus enabling efficient use of available bandwidth. The transmission path in a packet-switched network is always shared, not dedicated for a single use. As a result, once the packets are sent, the transmission path is once again available for transfer of other information. On the other hand, as discussed above, a circuit-switched network requires the establishment of a dedicated transmission path, which must be reserved in advance for the duration of the call. Once the dedicated circuit is reserved for transporting signals between two users, the circuit remains unavailable for other data or information transmission even if the circuit remains mostly idle during the course of the circuit connection.

Through the packet-switching nodes, packet-switching networks direct the flow of packets through the network until the packets reach the destination terminal. Once the packets are disseminated into the network, the packets travel to the first node in bursts on a first-come, first-served basis. Each individual packet contains a packet header, which identifies the source address and the destination address of the packets enabling the network to transfer each packet independently from source to the destination terminal. Upon arrival at each node, the packets are stored briefly so that the next routing decision can be made and then the packets are transmitted to the next leg of the transmission. The packets continue to follow the same process until they reach the final destination terminal.

As noted above, in packet-switched networks, data is transmitted in a series of packets. The packets contain user information and other networking instructions that enable the nodes to devise an efficient transmission path for the packets. Information used in the network internally for sequencing, routing control, flow control, and error control is encapsulated in each of the packets. Each packet, therefore, is a block of bits arranged in a particular format. Within each packet, a packet header, user information, destination and source address information, flow control information, and error control information are available to execute switching functions. Routing control information in each packet enables accurate routing of the information through the networks. Flow control information in the packet prevents packet switches from being congested in the transmission pathways. Complex error control procedures ensure error-free transmission of the packets. Additionally, each packet transmission contains additional processing information at the destination source to detect errors in transmission and to recover lost packets.

All of these functions are embedded in the packet header, which contains sufficient procedures for synchronization, routing, and sequencing of a transmitted data packet or frame. Each transmission requires the execution of routing decisions for each packet as it travels through and reaches the various switches within the network. This approach is different than circuit-switched networks in that the routing decisions are made before transmitting the signals within the network. As a result, the overhead needed in packet-switching technologies to execute routing, flow control, and error control functions reduces the amount of text or information that can be transmitted in a single packet. Wasted transmission bandwidth and packet overhead are some of the disadvantages of packet-switched networks, but as discusseed in the following paragraphs, evolution in networking schemes has limited these disadvantages to a minimum.

Packet-switched networks utilize two fundamental approaches to transfer the packets through the network: datagram and virtual circuit. In the datagram or connectionless packet-switching approach, each packet is routed independently to the destination address with the help of the networking instructions encapsulated in the packet header. As a result, it is possible that: (i) the various packets might traverse different paths through the network while traveling to the destination address even though all of the packets carry the same destination address, (ii) each of the packets may arrive at the destination address at different times, (iii) each of the packets may arrive at the destination address in different order or sequence, and (iv) individual packets might be destroyed or lost during the transmission.

The second approach, called virtual circuit packet-switching, is a connection-oriented system that involves the establishment of a fixed transmission path across the network before information can be transferred. As in circuit-switching networks, the call setup procedure typically requires the setting up of a transmission path and the allocation of resources along the pre-determined transmission path for the duration of the connection. Once the network identifies the transmission path for the packets, all of the packets traverse the same path through the network until they reach the final destination terminal. In a virtual circuit-switching scheme, it is not necessary for each packet to contain the full address of the source and the destination. As a result, virtual circuit-switching requires significantly less packet overhead and wastes less transmission bandwidth than datagram switching systems. The datagram approach, for example, does not allocate resources in advance, and, as a result, each packet contains comprehensive network instructions that help the network route individual packets to the destination address.

Frame Relay and ATM

Frame relay is a network interface protocol that builds upon technological developments in packet-switching schemes and upon improvements in transmission facilities generally. As network systems and transmission facilities improved over the years, error correction requirements became less stringent in switching schemes. The older networks were subject to transmission errors and, as a result, packet-switching techniques required a considerable amount of packet overhead to compensate for such error control and error detection functions. With the technological developments in networking schemes, today's transmission facilities operate with lower errors and, more importantly, modern transmission facilities have improved their abilities to detect and recover from transmission errors. As a result of this technological evolution, significant amounts of packet overhead, necessary in the past, are now unnecessary. The packets no longer require additional bits to detect and recover from transmission errors and less overhead is therefore built into the packets, which leads to higher utilization of available bandwidth within the network.

As noted above, frame relay is a fast packet-switching technology that takes advantage of technological advances in today's operating environment because it provides mostly digital, reliable, broadband equipment with high data rates and nearly error-free transmission. Frame relay uses variable-length packets, called frames, to transfer units of information within the packet-switched network. In combination with nearly error-free transmission facilities and sophisticated end-user systems that have sufficient error detection, error control, and error recovery capabilities, it is possible in frame relay technology to remove most of the header information that deals with transmission errors.

Further technological advances in networking schemes led to the development of Asynchronous Transfer Mode (ATM) networks, also referred to as cell relay, which supersedes the technology of frame relay networks generally. ATM is a connection-oriented switching technology that builds upon the evolution, and development of, circuit-switching and packet-switching technologies. ATM blends fast packet-switching and multiplexing techniques to create a process of information transfer in the form of fixed length packets or cells. In other words, ATM networks convert all user information into fixed-length packets, called cells. Each cell consists of an information field and a header, which determine the transmission path within the network. Frame relay, on the other hand, uses variable-length packets, called frames. As with frame relay, however, ATM networks require less overhead in packets for functions such as error control and error detection.

As with virtual circuit packet-switching technology, ATM networks require the setting up of a connection path before transferring the information through the network. As a connection-oriented network, ATM networks identify and allocate in advance sufficient switching and multiplexing capacity within the network to devise a transmission path through the network. In ATM schemes, bandwidth capacity and allocation of resources can be assigned for a designated information transfer on demand. Furthermore, ATM networks offer quality of service guarantees and flexible bandwidth on demand.

Transmission Systems

A transmission system is a very important component within a telecommunications network because it defines the communication path for transporting information from one node to another. In general, transmission facilities provide the communication paths that transport voice, data, and other network control information between users within the telecommunication network. Transmission facilities consist of a transmission medium and various types of electronic equipment located at points along the transmission route that amplify or regenerate signals, provide termination functions at points where transmission facilities connect to switching systems, and provide the means to combine many separate sets of call information into a single "multiplexed" signal to enhance transmission efficiency.

Transmission Medium

A transmission medium is any material substance or "free space," *i.e.*, a vacuum, that can be used for the propagation of energy in the form of pulses or variations in voltage, current, or light from one point to another; unguided in the case of free space or gaseous media, or guided by a boundary of material substance. Guided media, including paired metallic wire cable, coaxial cable, and fiber optic cable, constrain electromagnetic or acoustical waves within boundaries established by their physical construction. Unguided media is that in which boundary effects between free space and material substances are absent. The free space medium may include a gas or vapor. Unguided media including the atmosphere and outer space support terrestrial and satellite radio and optical transmission.

A. Guided Media

The various high-speed Internet access technologies currently offered by telecommunications companies fit into three broad categories of transmission modes: twisted-pair copper telephone wires, optical fiber, and fixed-wireless broadband. For decades, the most common medium-supporting voice applications within residential and business premises, *i.e.*, within the local loop, had been copper unshielded twisted pair ("UTP"). UTP is basically two wood-pulp or plastic-insulated copper wires (conductors), twisted together into a pair. The twists, or lays, are varied in length to reduce the potential for signal interference between pairs. Wire sizes range from 26 to 19 AWG (American Wire Gauge, *i.e.*, 0.016 to 0.036 inch in diameter), and are manufactured in cables consisting of 2 to 3600 pairs. A cable is a group of metallic conductors or optical fibers that are bound together, with a protective sheath, a strength member, and insulation between individual conductors/fibers, and contained within a jacket for the entire group.

In electrical circuits, a conductor is any material that readily permits a flow of electrons (electrical current). In twisted pair, the electrical signal wave propagates from the sending end to the receiving end in the dielectric material (insulation) between the two conductors. Due to the finite conductivity of copper, the medium for guided wave transmission is fundamentally dispersive. With dispersion, complex signals are distorted because the various frequency components which make up the signal have different propagation characteristics and paths.

Shielded twisted pair ("STP") cable is similar to UTP, but the twisted pairs are surrounded by an additional metallic sheath before being clad with an insulating jacket.

Coaxial cable consists of an insulated central copper or aluminum conductor surrounded by an outer metallic sheath that is clad with an insulating jacket. The outer sheath consists of copper tubing or braid. Coaxial cable with solid metallic outer sheaths reduces leakage of signals relative to braid-type designs. Because of its strength characteristics, cable television distribution systems normally use aluminum coaxial cable with solid outer sheaths to minimize radio frequency interference ("RFI") with aircraft navigation and other life safety systems.

Cables and other media differ in the following ways:

- Bandwidth capabilities (for example the number of voice conversations or data transfer that can be supported per circuit)
- Susceptibility to electrical interference from other communications circuits or from unrelated electrical machinery or natural sources such as lightning
- The ability to handle either analog or digital signals
- Cost

With UTP, one pair is commonly used for each voice conversation. However, with multiplexing schemes, UTP has been adapted to support 24-voice grade analog signals per pair. Coaxial cable, on the other hand, exhibits useful bandwidths in the hundreds of MHz (1 MHz = 1,000,000 hertz or cycles per second = one megahertz), and certain cables are able to transmit several thousand voice channels. Because it is considerably more expensive per foot than UTP, applications for coaxial cable predominantly require large bandwidths such as multiple channel voice, cable television, image transfer, and high-speed data networks.

Optical fibers are composed of concentric cylinders made of dielectric materials, *i.e.*, nonmetallic materials that do not conduct electricity. At the center is a core comprising the glass or plastic strand or fiber in which the lightwave travels. Cladding surrounds the core and is itself enclosed in a light-absorbing jacket that prevents interference among multi-fiber cables.

The optical fiber medium requires that electrical signals be converted to light signals for transmission through hair-thin strands of glass or plastic to light-sensitive receivers, where light signals are converted back to electrical signals. Some present and future technologies might eventually permit cost-competitive signal processing, filtering, switching, and multiplexing to occur in the optical-versus-electrical signal domain.

Optical fibers are either single mode or multimode. Multimode fibers, with much wider cores, allow the electromagnetic wave (lightwave) to enter at various angles, and reflect off core-cladding boundaries as light propagates from transmitter to receiver. Single-mode fibers have sufficiently small core diameters that the lightwaves are constrained to travel in only one transverse path from transmitter to receiver. This requires the utmost in angular alignment of light-emitting devices at points where light enters the fiber, and it results in higher transmitter/termination costs than multimode fiber systems.

From a technical performance point of view, single mode fiber exhibits band-widths of up to 100,000 MHz while multimode bandwidth is in the range of 1,000 to 2,000 MHz (1,000 MHz = one billion hertz = one gigahertz = 1 GHz).

The principal advantages of lightwave transmission using fiber optic cable (also referred to as lightguide) are ultra-wide bandwidth, small size and weight, low attenuation relative to comparable metallic media (attenuation is signal level or amplitude loss per foot of length), and virtual immunity to interference from electrical machinery and man-made or natural atmospheric electrical disturbances. Disadvantages include the added cost for electro-optical transmitters and detectors, higher termination costs (largely manpower for making physical connections and splices), and overall higher installed cost in short distance applications such as premises wiring systems.

Advantages outweigh the disadvantages, however, and fiber optic cable is rapidly becoming the transmission medium of choice in applications such as high-capacity multichannel metropolitan and wide area interoffice trunks, transoceanic cables, and high-speed data communications. In addition, decreasing costs have resulted in fiber optic penetration into the realm of premises wiring. This is occurring in enterprises that require wide bandwidth communications among campus buildings and/or directly to desktops for specialized applications, such as image file transfer.

B. Unguided Media

Unguided media, that is the atmosphere and outer space, is used in terrestrial microwave radio transmission systems, satellite, mobile telephone, and personal communications systems. Terrestrial microwave radio transmission systems consist of, at least, two radio transmitter/receivers (transceivers) connected to high-gain antennas (directional antennas that concentrate electromagnetic or radiowave energy in narrow beams) focused in pairs on each other. The operation is point-to-point. In other words, communications can be established between only two installations. This is contrasted to point-to-multipoint systems, such as broadcast radio or citizen band radios.

In long-distance carrier applications, terrestrial microwave is an alternative to guided metallic or fiber optic cable transmission media. For this application, antennas are normally mounted on towers and require an unobstructed or line-of-sight path between the antennas, which typically can be separated by up to 30 miles. Strings of intermediate or relay towers, each with at least two antennas and repeater/transceivers to detect and amplify signals, interconnect switching centers in different metropolitan locations.

One advantage of terrestrial microwave is that it obviates the need to acquire right-of-ways (except for towers) or to bury cable or construct aerial facilities. In areas where the cost of right-of-ways is very high or in some rural areas where cable installation costs might be prohibitive, significant savings can be realized with microwave. However, as a transmission medium, the earth's atmosphere creates problems not encountered with other media. For example, trees, obstructions, heavy ground fog, rain, and very cold air over warm terrain can cause significant attenuation or signal power loss. Decades of experience have led to conservative tower spacing, space and frequency diversity (alternate physical paths and frequencies), and other engineering practices to offset these difficulties and achieve reliable operation. Another problem associated with microwave transmission is the possible inability to obtain operating licenses due to dense usage and the associated frequency congestion in a number of metropolitan areas.

Commercial satellite communication entails microwave radio, line-of-sight propagation from a transmitting earth terminal (usually ground-based, but potentially ship- or airborne) through free space (the atmosphere and outer space) media to a satellite, and back again to earthbound receiving terminals. Terminals, sometimes termed "earth stations," consist of antennas and electronics necessary to:

- Interface satellite equipment with terrestrial systems
- Modulate and demodulate radio frequency ("RF") carrier signals with multiple (multiplexed) voice and data signals
- Transmit and receive RF carrier signals to and from satellites
- Otherwise establish, support and control communications among earth terminals

In essence, satellites are equivalent to orbiting microwave repeaters.

High-Speed Transmission Links

The various high-speed Internet access technologies currently offered by telecommunications companies fit into three broad categories of transmission modes: twisted-pair copper telephone wires, optical fiber, and fixed-wireless broadband. Cost and availability of varies from market to market. The sections below briefly describe each technology. Before beginning, however, a bit of basic background vocabulary will be useful to the average reader. For starters, bandwidth means capacity to transmit data in bits per second. Traditionally, communication channels were called bands. Technologists refer to the existing voice networks, which transmit information at rates below 56 Kbps (kilo bits per second), as narrowband. Anything faster than 56 Kbps, but slower than 1.5 Mbps (mega bits per second), is referred to as wideband, and anything faster than 1.5 Mbps is referred to as broadband.

A. Digital Subscriber Line Technology Using Copper Wires

Digital Subscriber Line (DSL) technology deploys broadband services by increasing the availability of bandwidth on a building's existing copper wire network. DSL services use existing telephone lines to provide continuous "always-on" connection to the Internet without causing busy signals if other users are on the Internet. This multiple use of the copper wire is made possible by taking advantage of the unused frequency bands on the copper wire. While the voice traffic passes on the copper wire using audio frequencies, DSL utilizes digital signal processing technology to transfer bandwidth-intensive information at rates ranging from 1 to 3 Mbps. Technologists predict that, in the near future, certain types of DSL services will reach speeds of 5 to 15 Mbps, which are currently needed to achieve television-quality transmission.

Because DSL utilizes existing telephone lines, telecommunications companies can deploy DSL service quickly and without costly installation of higher-grade cable, although poor quality of existing building wires can impede performance. Additionally, critics have noted that DSL simply infuses a temporary breath of life to the outdated century-old copper infrastructure. Further capital and technological investments in existing copper wire networks is as short-sighted as patching a leaky roof and praying for sunshine; a complete replacement of the old copper infrastructure is the most sensible solution for the future.

B. Optical Fiber Technology

As described above, fiber-optic communications are based on the principle that light in a glass medium can carry information more quickly over longer distances than electrical signals can carry in a copper or coaxial medium. Whereas transmission over copper wires utilizes frequencies in the megahertz range, transmission over fiber utilizes frequencies a million times higher. This difference permits transmission of data over fiber lines at speeds as high as 10 gbps (gigabits per second). According to the International Engineering Consortium, at this speed the entire fifteen-volume set of Encyclopedia Britannica can be transmitted in well under one second.

Fiber-optic broadband connections are available through a number of sources and offer virtually unlimited bandwidth to the user willing to pay for it. For businesses, the cost of accessing fiber-optic connections is governed by the distance from the business to the fiber-optic network. In highly urbanized areas, several companies typically maintain fiber-optic lines or networks. As a result, fiber access in urban areas is more widely available and priced competitively. In less densely populated areas, however, fiber-optic connection is generally cost prohibitive, and perhaps unavailable.

C. Wireless Broadband

Wireless broadband includes a number of different technologies that range from fixed-point radio/microwave to satellite to laser. Currently, the business market is dominated by radio/microwave services that offer Internet connection speeds greater than 1.5 Mbps. Broadband providers are aggressively constructing wireless networks in different markets throughout the country, thus, dramatically expanding the wireless options available to both urban and rural end users. Once ballyhooed for its elegant solution to the lack of expensive fiber optic cables snaking in the cities, the fixed wireless industry is now badly in need of profits, capital, and respect. Some of the fixed wireless options currently available in the market are briefly described below:

1. MMDS (Multi-channel Multipoint Distribution Service)

MMDS technology operates at frequencies of 2.1 to 2.7 Gigahertz of the electromagnetic spectrum. Signals sent using MMDS can travel from point to point up to 40 miles before needing to be boosted.

2. ISM (Industrial Scientific Medical)

ISM technology operates at frequencies of 2.4 to 5.8 Gigahertz of the electromagnetic spectrum. Signals sent through using ISM technology can travel from point to point from 5 to 25 miles before needing to be boosted. This technology is utilized to supplement MMDS within a local service area. ISM provides access to the Internet at similar rates to that of MMDS.

3. LMDS (Local Multipoint Distribution System)

LMDS technology operates at frequencies of 28 to 31 Gigahertz of the electromagnetic spectrum. Signals using LMDS technology can travel from point to point up to 3 miles before needing to be boosted. Carriers using LMDS are building wireless rings offering service in urban areas. LMDS provides access to the Internet at rates up to 11 Mbps.

4. Millimeter Wave

Millimeter Wave technology operates at frequencies of 28 to 38 Gigahertz of the electromagnetic spectrum. Signals using Millimeter Wave technology can travel from point to point from 1 to 3 miles before needing to be boosted. Millimeter Wave provides access to the Internet at rates up to 11 Mbps.

5. Satellite Technology

Satellite Internet access is currently limited due to the fact that signals can only be beamed down to the user but cannot be transmitted back from the user to the satellite. Nevertheless, by using a separate analog Internet service provider connection over a telephone line to send signals upstream, users can gain the benefit of high-speed downstream transmissions via satellite broadband. For users who require bandwidth primarily for the purposes of receiving data from the Internet, satellite technology offers an excellent and affordable solution. Two-way satellite communication networks are currently under development by both Spaceway (Hughes) and Teledesic.

6. Laser-based Broadband Technology

Laser-based broadband technology is currently under development by Lucent and TeraBeam Networks. Laser has the advantage of being able to transmit data at even higher speeds than LMDS and Millimeter Wave technology, and can be used to access remote areas. However, laser performance can be impaired by harsh weather or heavy fog. Because laser broadband is not currently available on a widespread basis, it is difficult to evaluate its advantages or disadvantages thoroughly.

CHAPTER 4

Installation and Commissioning

Before installation commences, it is vital that the service provider conducts proper due diligence of the building. The provider should concentrate on determining the feasibility and cost-effectiveness of installing communications services in the building. Special attention should be paid to the types of tenants in the building to determine if demand exists for such services.

Entry and Access

A typical access agreement provides the telecommunications company certain rights to access and to utilize the building's riser space and/or roof space in order to connect the company's telecommunications equipment and cables to the building tenants. The riser space and/or the roof space are used by the telecommunications company for installing and then operating the telecommunications equipment and cables through which the company provides services to the building's tenants. The company either provides these services directly or connects to other telecommunications service providers who, in turn, provide services to the building tenants. Accordingly, the telecommunications company could serve as (i) the telecommunications carrier for the building tenants, or (ii) the carrier's carrier for other telecommunications company with access rights in the building.

A telecommunications company should always negotiate the broadest use clause possible. Possible innovations in transmission technologies or future evolution in the company's business structure are just some of the reasons why a telecommunications company might switch from one transmission technology to the other in delivering broadband services to building tenants. The telecommunications company, in this context, requires the flexibility to change or supplement the transmission mode technology it uses to deliver the broadband services to tenants, particularly when better techonology and equipment become available. For example, a company that deploys proprietary, in-building fiber optics infrastructure to transmit broadband and other services to tenants might want the flexibility to switch to fixed wireless transmission mode. Such flexibility in switching or supplementing transmission technologies might be necessary to take advantage of future cost savings inherent in one technology over the other.

Another example would be that switching to a different transmission mode might be necessary because of a corporate merger or acquisition. A company may also have a limited range of broadband services that it is capable of providing with its choice of transmission technology. In order to expand its businesses into other areas or even change businesses, the company may have to switch to a different transmission infrastructure. Finally, the telecommunications company's ability to later assign the license agreement also may depend upon whether the use clause is sufficiently broad. The challenge for the counsel who advises telecommunications companies, therefore, is to negotiate a broad use provision which anticipates possible economic, legal, and operational problems that may arise during the term of the agreement.

There are, however, several situations where it is in the best interest of the building owner to place use restrictions upon the telecommunications company and limit the scope of "permitted services."

Permitted Services and Use Restrictions

While restricting the service provider's ability to deliver additional telecommunications services that are not within the scope of "Permitted Services" is helpful, it might be practically difficult for building owners to monitor the service provider's compliance with such use restrictions. A service provider can circumvent these use restrictions by installing additional equipment in the building and providing additional services to building occupants without alerting the building owner of its breach. The building owner's only preventive measure might be to restrict the service provider's ability to install additional equipment without obtaining the building owner's consent.

Accordingly, the agreement should not only list the various "Permitted Services" or "Services" that the telecommunications service providers are entitled to deliver to the building's occupants, it should also contain use restrictions that prohibit certain actions. The agreement, for example, should require the service provider to obtain the building owner's approval and pay reasonable consideration before the service provider is able to use the building as a telecommunications hub. The rationale behind this restriction is simple—the service provider should not use the building as a hub to deliver services to other buildings in the vicinity. In addition to restricting the service provider's ability to generate income from other buildings in the area, the agreement should restrict the service provider's ability to generate additional telecommunications revenues from the building itself by co-locating its equipment with other telecommunications companies. A well-crafted access agreement, which allows a service provider to co-locate its equipment with other telecommunications companies, in essence, wrestles control over the building's telecommunications facilities from the building owner to the service provider. By co-locating equipment with other telecommunications companies, the service provider is able to compete with the building owner for future telecommunications revenues generated from the building. For example, if future negotiations with the building owner fail, the other telecommunications companies could reach a co-location agreement with the original service provider and bypass the building owner in gaining access to the building's telecommunication facilities.

The following are sample use restrictions that address these important points:

> Licensee shall use commercially reasonable efforts to ensure that no contractors or employees of Licensee with insufficient training, expertise or experience enter the Telecom Space or Licensor's riser or equipment closets for the purpose of installing, inspecting, operating, maintaining or removing the Telecom Equipment. Licensee shall not (i) provide telecommunications services to customers in other buildings from the Telecom Space, unless expressly authorized in the Permitted Services, (ii) permit co-location, i.e., permit anyone other than Licensee or its employees, contractors, or agents to use any portion of the Telecom Space unless such occupant has entered into a separate access or license agreement with Licensor, or (iii) replace or augment any component of the Telecom Equipment in order to provide additional services to Students not expressly included in Permitted Services (as opposed to replacing obsolete or defective Telecom Equipment or upgrading technology to provide the same services more efficiently or to improve the quality of the same services), without the prior written consent of Licensor. Licensor may condition its consent for Licensee to do any of the foregoing upon (A) the execution of a new license agreement, and/or (B) the payment by Licensee of additional fees.

> Licensor shall have the right to enter into any agreement containing any terms with any telecommunications service provider ("TSP") to provide any telecommunications service to the Building, including any one or more of the Permitted Services. Pro-

vided such TSPs have previously entered into currently existing license agreements with Licensor for access to the Building, Licensee shall have the right to enter into agreements with such TSPs granting them the right, on a non-exclusive basis, to utilize the Telecom Equipment in such TSPs' provision of services to the Tenants and, where necessary in connection with the provision of such services, to install and maintain telecommunications equipment in the Equipment Area.

Except as otherwise provided in this Agreement, (i) Licensee shall not provide any services to Tenants unless such services are also available to such Tenants from other telecommunications service providers, (ii) Licensee shall not provide any services to any Tenant that it does not also provide to other customers who are not Tenants, (iii) any services provided by Licensee to a Tenant will not be customized to fit the specific needs of such Tenant, (iv) this Agreement is a bona fide agreement, negotiated at arm's length between Licensor and Licensee, and is of a type customarily entered into by building owners and service providers in the geographic area in which the Building is located, (v) the services offered or provided by Licensee to Tenants, will be selected by Tenants from a menu of services, all of which are generally available to other customers of Licensee, and (vi) Licensee shall not provide any services to Tenants of the Building unless such services are of the type which are customarily rendered to tenants of commercial office properties in the geographic areas in which that Building is located.

The rest of this chapter looks at the issues involved in designing and installing a cabling system.

Guidelines for Designing and Installing a Cabling System

A reliable, standards-based, flexible cabling system that supports high-speed technologies is the foundation of any in-building broadband telecommunications network. A structured-cabling system consists of properly labeled and marked, high-quality cables and cabling components that are installed properly using common industry-wide structured-cabling standards. In order to maximize efficiency, the building's cabling system must be capable of accommodating future customer demands and technological innovations. At a very minimum, in-building telecommunications networks should support both voice and data communications. Planning ahead by designing a unified cabling system that can support both voice and data communications is ideal.

Planning that anticipates the future needs of building tenants is efficient and cost effective in the long run. For example, installing just enough cables to accommodate the current needs of building tenants will most likely require additional recurring investments in the building's cabling infrastructure as demands on data cabling to support higher speed technologies continue to increase. In addition to building a cabling system that can support future technologies, the design and the installation of the cabling system must be reliable. Most network failures occur because in-building telecommunications infrastructure consists of inferior cables and cable components that were improperly installed. Troubleshooting cabling systems that are poorly designed using inferior installation techniques, with no clear labels or markings, can be expensive for both building owners and telecommunications companies.

A poorly planned and poorly implemented cabling system can cause intermittent or permanent problems ranging from slow access times to complete network failures. Poor installation can also aggravate conditions that create electrical interference with the network from outside sources. An unreliable cabling system is typically more susceptible to intermittent network problems and, as a result, end users will most likely experience problems with dropped or lost packets. When packets are dropped or lost, the transmitted data either never arrives at the desired destination or arrives in an incomplete format. In order to avoid network problems incident to shoddy installation techniques, the building owner must require the telecommunications company to follow stringent design specifications and to use high-quality cables and cable components. For example, to avoid electrical interference, the communications cables or wires should not be placed in any raceway, compartment, outlet box, junction box, or similar fitting with any conductors of electrical power.

Typically, the telecommunications company is financially and technically responsible for the purchase, installation, maintenance, and repair of the hardware required to provide telecommunications services to a building. The building owner determines the physical space within the building where the telecommunications company will be permitted to install the telecommunications equipment, and generally allows the company to install the telecommunications cabling in the available riser space behind the walls. The equipment is typically installed in the equipment room located on the first floor of the building or on the building's rooftop, depending on the type of transmission media that the company uses to deploy the in-building broadband services. In addition to providing the physical space in the equipment room or on the rooftop, the building owner makes available the necessary wiring and connections, electrical power and sockets and cooling facilities that the telecommunications company needs to deploy its services.

From a building owner's standpoint, the telecommunications company's obligations relating to the installation, maintenance, repair and operation of the telecommunications equipment and cabling should be precisely defined. Prior to commencing any work relating to the construction, installation or material modification of any telecommunications equipment within the building, the agreement should require the telecommunications company to submit detailed specifications, plans and drawings relating to the cable installation work. The building owner's review of the plans and drawings must focus on whether the proposed installation or construction work will affect the building's aesthetic appearance, structural integrity or mechanical, plumbing, electrical, heating, ventilation, air conditioning, life safety or other building systems. Moreover, the building owner should determine whether any of the telecommunications equipment would affect other areas or equipment in the building due to heat loads. Finally, the building owner should seek assurance from the telecommunications company that the proposed construction or installation work will not create any environmental concerns.

A sample provision which deals with guidelines for the installation, maintenance, repair, and restoration of the cabling system follows:

Modification or Installation of Telecom Space or System. Before installing or modifying any System or connecting any Resident to the System, Company shall deliver to Owner for review and approval final plans and specifications (collectively, the "Installation Plans") setting forth in detail the design, location, size, weight, material composition, method of installation and, if applicable, frequency of the System, and proposed Horizontal and Vertical Designated Routes, together with evidence reasonably satisfactory to Owner that the Installation Plans comply with the Operating Requirements (defined below). De minimus modifications to the System or plans shall not require the approval of Owner. Owner's approval of the Installation Plans shall not constitute a representation or warranty by Owner that the Installation Plans comply with the Operating Requirements. Company's installation of the System in the Telecom Space, or connection of any Resident thereto, shall not commence without (a) Owner's prior written approval of the Installation Plans and all contractors, subcontractors and materials suppliers which Company proposes to employ, and (b) receipt by Owner of true and correct copies of Company's licenses and permits for operation and installation of the System. Company agrees to use Owner's designated cabling contractor for the installation of cabling in the risers located within the Premises and for connections to Residents provided that such designated contractor's rates are reasonable. The installation and/or connection shall be performed (i) at the sole cost of Company, (ii) in a good and workmanlike manner, (iii) in accordance with the Installation Plans, all the Operating Requirements, and the instructions of Owner (and any outside consultant employed by Owner), and (iv) without interfering with the use of any portion of the Premises by Owner or the Residents.

Company's Covenants. Company covenants and agrees as follows:

(a) Operating Requirements. Company shall, at Company's expense, perform all acts necessary to ensure that Company, the System (including installation, maintenance, operation and removal), and the Telecom Space are at all times in compliance with the following defined items, as the same may be amended from time to time (collectively, the "Operating Requirements"), and will Indemnify and Defend the Owner Parties against all Claims arising from any failure by a Company Party, the System or the Telecom Space to comply with the Operating Requirements:

(i) "Applicable Law": to the extent the same affect Owner, Company, the Telecom Space, any System, the Premises or this Agreement: (A) laws, rulings, orders, regulations, restrictions or requirements currently in effect or adopted in the future by any governmental entity, including licensing, zoning, building and fire codes, and rules, regulations and orders of the Federal Communications Commission and Federal Aviation Agency, or (B) easements, requirements, standards or restrictions currently in effect or adopted in the future by any board of fire underwriters, insurance carrier, utility company, Premises owner's association or similar body or imposed by a land owner.

(ii) "Rules and Regulations": the rules and regulations promulgated by Owner for the Premises.

(iii) "Technical Standards": the technical standards attached to this Agreement as Exhibit "__", as modified from time to time by Owner. If any new Technical Standards established by Owner require Company to modify, renovate or revise the then-existing installation, operation or maintenance of the System, Company shall make such modifications or revisions, at Company's expense, within a reasonable time thereafter, not to exceed sixty (60) days after receipt of written notice.

(b) <u>Condition of System; Repairs</u>. Company shall (i) maintain and operate the System in a good and safe condition; (ii) keep the Telecom Space in a safe condition and free from all trash, debris and waste resulting from its use by Company; and (iii) repair all damage to the Telecom Space and/or the Premises occurring in connection with the installation, use, maintenance, relocation or removal of the System. If Company fails to perform any of the foregoing obligations within five (5) business days after receipt of Owner's notice of such failure by Company, Owner may perform such obligations on Company's behalf, and Company shall reimburse Owner for all reasonable costs incurred in connection therewith (plus 15% for Owner's administrative costs) within fifteen (15) days after receipt of Owner's invoice. Company's reimbursement obligation shall survive the expiration or earlier termination of this Agreement. Owner shall have no responsibility for maintaining any portion of the Telecom Space.

(c) <u>Costs; Liens</u>. Company shall pay or cause to be paid all costs for work performed or materials provided by or at the direction of Company and/or related to the System or the Telecom Space. Company shall, within ten (10) days after receipt of notice from Owner, discharge or bond around any mechanic's or materialmen's lien attributable to the performance of such work or provision of such materials.

(d) <u>Surrender of Space</u>.

(i) <u>Removal of Telecom Equipment</u>. Upon expiration or earlier termination of this Agreement, Licensee shall remove from the Property all of the Removable Equipment (defined below) and peaceably surrender the Telecom Space to Licensor in the same condition the Telecom Space was in on the Effective Date, except (A) ordinary wear and tear and (B) if termination resulted from a Casualty, damage not required to be repaired by Licensee. Prior to the expiration of this Agreement or in connection with a termination of this Agreement, Licensor may notify Licensee in writing which cable and conduit Licensee will be required to remove. Any cable or conduit not so designated by Licensor will not be removed by Licensee and will become the property of Licensor. All Telecom Equipment which Licensee is required to remove is referred to as the "Removable Equipment."

(ii) <u>Failure to Remove</u>. If Licensee fails to remove the Removable Equipment from the Property within ten (10) days after the expiration or earlier termination of Licensee's right to use the

Telecom Space, Licensor may remove and store or dispose of any remaining Removable Equipment in any manner Licensor deems appropriate. Licensee shall reimburse Licensor for all costs incurred by Licensor in connection therewith within thirty (30) days after Licensor's request (plus 10% to cover Licensor's administrative costs). In addition, if Licensee fails to remove the Removable Equipment from the Telecom Space after the expiration or earlier termination of this Agreement without executing a new Agreement, Licensee shall, at the option of Licensor, be deemed in holdover subject to all provisions of this Agreement except that the term of the holdover will be month to month and the Net Revenues shall be three hundred fifty percent (350%) of the quarterly Net Revenues for the last quarter of the Term.

The access agreement must contain a clear and unambiguous description of not only the physical space in the equipment room where equipment and hardware will be located but also those spaces behind the walls in which voice and data cabling will be installed. The agreement should contain, therefore, a clear description of the horizontal and vertical pathways in the riser space, designating the routes through which the cables will run from the equipment room to the work area. In addition to defining the equipment room and the cable pathways, the agreement should define the equipment that the telecommunications company proposes to install within the building. Sample definitions of equipment and the equipment room follows:

> "Equipment Room" shall mean the space in the Building of not more than sixty (60) square feet in the location designated by Licensor and shown on the attached Exhibit, which space shall be the location for items of Licensee's Equipment, as such Licensee's Equipment may be installed, replaced, supplemented, maintained, repaired, relocated, upgraded or substituted by Licensee from time to time in accordance with this Agreement. Licensor shall have no obligation to enclose, demise, or provide any security with respect to the Equipment Room or Licensee's Equipment.
>
> or
>
> "Equipment Room": Subject to availability: approximately __ square feet of space within reasonable proximity to the Property's main telecommunications room located on the _____ level or floor of the Property. The exact location of the Equipment Area will be designated by Licensor within _____ (__) days after receipt of written request from Licensee and will be subject to the

approval of Licensee. If the designated Equipment Area is unacceptable to Licensee, Licensor agrees to act in good faith and cooperate with Licensee to locate an alternative location that is reasonably acceptable to both Licensee and Licensor. If no Equipment Area is available or if the space available for the Equipment Area is unacceptable to Licensee, this Agreement will terminate immediately upon receipt of written notice by Licensee that no Equipment Area is available or receipt of written notice by Licensor that Licensee finds the available space to be unacceptable. If the space for Equipment Area is available and reasonably acceptable to Licensee, the parties will execute an amendment to this Agreement attaching Exhibit "A" (floor plan) and Exhibit "B" (Property cross section) showing the exact location of the Equipment Area and Cable Pathways.

"Cable Pathways": Horizontal and vertical paths for Licensee's Cable (hereinafter defined) from entry into the Property to the Equipment Area, all as illustrated on Exhibit "A" and Exhibit "B" to be attached to this Agreement upon determination of the exact location of the Equipment Area. Licensee will have no right to utilize the Property's riser space to connect to any Student (hereinafter defined) or other TSP (hereinafter defined) without expressly describing the riser space to be utilized and including such riser space within the definition of "Cable Pathways."

"Equipment" shall mean equipment used for the transmission of communications services including (without limitation) servers, racks, cabinets, cables, junction boxes, hangers, pull boxes, innerducts, connecting equipment, termination blocks, electrical wiring and related equipment, or any components thereof.

A lawyer advising either building owners or telecommunications companies must understand the design characteristics of a typical, structured cabling infrastructure. Provisions dealing with installation, maintenance, repair and restoration of the in-building broadband network must address technical, legal and operational issues that might surface during the term of the agreement. With a clear understanding of the design topology for the building's cabling system, a lawyer will be able to negotiate and then memorialize adequate safeguards that anticipate network, safety and other construction-related problems.

In most structured cabling infrastructure, the cabling system originates at the demarcation point, travels to the equipment room, cross-connects vertically to the telecommunications closet, and then cross-connects again horizontally to reach the last leg of the transmission leading to the work area. The point within a building where the telecommunications company's wiring terminates and where the customer's wiring and equipment originates is called the demarcation point. The demarcation point divides the respective maintenance and operation rights and responsibilities between the telecommunications company and the building owner, with the telecommunications company being responsible for the facility up to the demarcation point and the building owner being responsible for the equipment and inside cabling beyond the demarcation point. Sample definitions of a demarcation point follow:

> "Licensee Demarcation Point" shall mean a location defined by any Laws, contract or custom where an incumbent local exchange carrier or a competitive local exchange carrier terminates its network within the Building.
> "Tenant Demarcation" shall mean the interface point between customer premises equipment of user Tenants, located within a Building, and Licensee's Equipment.

From the demarcation point, the cabling infrastructure travels to the equipment room located on the first floor or the basement of the building. The equipment room is a secure, temperature-controlled, centralized location within the building which houses routers, switches, hubs and other telephone and data-networking equipment. The equipment room typically has wide entrance areas and high ceilings to accommodate the large equipment that it houses. It is also the location where backbone cabling terminates.

Backbone cabling, which is also known as vertical cabling or riser cabling, is the vertical connection for the entrance facility, the equipment rooms and the telecommunications closets. Telecommunications closets, also known as wiring closets, intermediate cross-connects, or intermediate distribution frames, are remote locations within buildings where the horizontal structured cabling leading to the work areas originates and backbone cabling originating from the equipment rooms terminates. In other words, the telecommunications closet is the location where the backbone cabling and the horizontal cabling cross-connects. In a multi-story building, it is ideal to have at least one telecommunications closet for each floor. In a telecommunications closet, one can find not only cabling components such as cross-connects and patch panels but also phone systems, power protection, uninterruptible power supplies, networking equipment such as local area network hubs, switches, routers and repeaters and file servers and data-processing equipment. Within the cabling system, cross-connect serves as a link in the cabling chain that permits the termination of a cabling line and reconnection of that cabling line to another line using jumpers, termination blocks and/or other cables. Sample definition provisions describing telephone closets and horizontal and vertical cables follow:

> "Telephone Closets" shall mean locations designated by Licensor within any Building at which interconnections between Lateral/Station Cables, Tenant Demarcations, Risers, Service Provider Demarcations and related components are made. Telephone closets may be located on each floor of a Building and may be designated by Licensor for common use by all communications service providers.
>
> "Lateral/Station Cables" are those cables located on a single floor of a Building that interconnect a Riser with a Service Provider Demarcation or a Tenant Demarcation within such Building.
>
> "Risers" shall mean the vertical portions or segments of the Cable.
>
> "Cable" shall be limited to unshielded or shielded twisted pair, copper wire, and related conduit and components necessary to deliver Communication Services from the Equipment Room to the Tenant Demarcation Point.

Cables are routed vertically from the equipment room to the telecommunications closet through a space called the riser. A riser is the vertical shaft between two floors in a multi-floor building through which cables are routed to connect telephone closets. From the telephone closet, horizontal cables are pulled through spaces between the structural ceiling and the drop ceiling or raised-floor spaces to connect the telecommunications closets and the work area. If these horizontal pathways serve as pathways for the return of air to the HVAC unit, the space is then called a "plenum." In essence, a plenum is a duct, raceway, or air space between either the false ceiling or the drop ceiling and the structural ceiling or a raised-floor space, which is used for returning air to the heating ventilation and air conditioning equipment. Horizontal cabling is typically installed and pulled through plenum spaces. The NEC requires that expensive plenum cable be used in these plenum spaces.

Horizontal cables, therefore, create the connection between a cross-connect panel within a telecommunications or a wiring closet and the wall jack in the work area. Backbone cabling, on the other hand, creates the vertical connection between the telecommunications or the wiring closet and the equipment room that houses the main cross-connect point of the building. The design specifications for these horizontal and vertical pathways must ensure that they are moisture-free spaces that are properly grounded to avoid electric shocks.

The access agreement should also require telecommunications companies to install cabling and equipment in a manner that will safeguard the cabling from damage caused by normal building use. To protect the cables within the horizontal and vertical pathways, individual cables are typically encased in either a conduit or a cable tray. A conduit is a metallic or non-metallic pipe (usually made of plastic) with a finite amount of space that runs from floor to floor connecting equipment rooms and telecommunications closets or along a floor or ceiling connecting the work area to a telecommunications closet. Cables are placed in these pipes to protect the cable from burning or generating visible smoke. An example of a conduit that is specifically designed to carry and protect optical-fiber cables are fiber-protection systems. Drafting specifications for construction of conduits must accommodate future growth, with enough vacant space for adding additional cables as need arises. Conduits are expensive to install and require lots of interfloor drilling. Therefore, construction provisions dealing with conduit installation should consider such issues as expense and overtime labor costs incident to noisy conduit drilling.

Unlike a conduit, which encases the cables in a pipe, a cable tray is a wire rack in which cable is laid or hung. One of the advantages of the open design of a cable tray is that the cables are accessible for both maintenance and troubleshooting. In buildings with walls made of brick or concrete, if telecommunications conduits have not been installed, a surface-mount raceway is used to carry cables. A raceway is a special type of a conduit that is mounted on the outside of a wall. Inner ducts, for example, are flexible, plastic raceways used to carry optical-fiber cables.

Lastly, the cabling system might contain hardware equipment called racks used to organize cabling infrastructure. There are three types of racks: (i) wall-mounted brackets that are used in tight areas with little available space, (ii) skeletal frames that have an open design, and (iii) full equipment cabinets that provide the best physical security, cooling, and protection against electromagnetic interference.

Although an in-building broadband infrastructure requires uninterrupted electrical support, a basic cabling system absorbs very little electricity. A typical cabling system requires electrical power that is supplied by a minimum of two dedicated 120V-20A nominal, nonswitched, AC-duplex electrical outlets, with each outlet connected to a separate branch circuit. As added precaution against an electrical power failure, the equipment room, the entrance facility, and all of the telecommunication closets should be equipped with adequate electrical surge suppression, uninterruptible power supply, and standby lighting to supply temporary AC power. Depending on the size and complexity of the broadband network, the parties may install submeters to measure consumption of electricity.

In-building Network and a Structured Cabling System

This section deals with achieving interconnectivity and interoperability among in-building telecommunications facilities. In any building, commercial or residential, transmission cables supporting data and voice communications are the foundation of any in-building telecommunications network. The importance of a reliable and well-designed structured cabling system for buildings, therefore, cannot be overstated. A building's cabling system carries not only data traffic across the building's telecommunications network, it can also be used to transport voice, security alarm signals, video and audio transmissions. Successful provisioning of these telecommunications facilities within buildings is largely dependent upon the interconnectivity and interoperability of those facilities. Achieving such interconnectivity and interoperability among the telecommunications facilities is not so easy, however. A typical telecommunications network inside a building or among a group of buildings, such as an office park or campus, is comprised of multiple telecommunications products and equipment, each manufactured and serviced by multiple vendors.

In a multiple product/vendor environment, interconnectivity and interoperability of these products and vendor specifications are cardinal objectives of any network design and installation. From a historical perspective, however, early cabling systems were unstructured, proprietary, and often worked only with a specific vendor's equipment. In the late 1980s and early 1990s, telecommunications traffic consisted of mostly analog or digital voice communications. Network engineers installed twisted-pair copper cabling in the buildings to transport such telephone transmissions. Demand for broadband communications became robust only in the late 1990s, and, as a result, for many previous years cable design and architecture remained relatively static. In the pre-broadband era, because the cabling systems were not required to support high-speed network applications, proprietary and vendor-specific cabling systems that lacked flexibility satisfied the average telecommunications customer. Vendor-specific cabling locked the customer into a proprietary system. For these customers, any upgrades of the existing telecommunications infrastructure or installation of new systems often required the construction of a completely new cabling infrastructure. Similarly, moves and changes often necessitated major cabling plant reconfigurations. Even as late as 1998, most of the buildings had several different types of cables snaking through the walls, floors and ceilings, and each cable met only the standards dictated by the particular vendor requiring a particular cable type.

Premises Distribution Systems

A premises distribution system ("PDS") is composed of wire, cable and other equipment necessary to link desktop terminals (workstation locations) with telephone switch, computer, image, video and other information hosts, and with external telecommunications networks. These hosts may all be located in a single building or distributed among multiple buildings in campus environments. The cable system extends from the workstation to the host port, enabling the telecommunications user to literally plug into the desired information channel. For many years, cable system architecture was relatively static. Technological advances, however, have created an environment in which cable system design and implementation is as critical as that of the voice, data, or video systems themselves.

Uniform wiring makes networks capable of supporting voice and data in multiple product/vendor environments, and minimizing the need for future modifications to accommodate user requirement changes or technology upgrades. These are the primary premises distribution system design objectives. This chapter deals with practical considerations gained from experience with previous approaches and focuses on PDS planning and implementation factors and techniques needed to achieve PDS objectives.

Standards-based Structured Cabling System

As the demand for broadband services became increased, it did not take long for industry experts, consumers and vendors to realize that a more comprehensive standard had to be developed to outline not only the types of cables that should be used but also the standards for deployment, connectors, patch panels, and more. Hoping to steer away from unstructured and proprietary cabling systems that only worked with a specific vendor's equipment, the telecommunications industry eventually developed a versatile standards-based approach to in-building network design. A consortium of telecommunications vendors and consultants worked in conjunction with the American National Standards Institute (ANSI), Electronic Industries Association (EIA), and the Telecommunications Industry Association (TIA) to create a standard originally known as the Commercial Building Telecommunications Cabling Standard or ANSI/EIA/TIA-568-1991. This standard has been revised and updated several times and is now known as ANSI/TIA/EIA-568-A or just TIA/EIA-568-A. In subsequent years TIA/EIA-568-A has been updated with a series of addenda.

Standards are basically agreements with industry-wide, national, and possibly international scope that allow equipment manufactured by different vendors to be interoperable. Standards focus on interfaces that specify how equipment is physically interconnected and what procedures are used to operate across different equipment. Standards applying to data communications between computers specify the hardware and software procedures through which computers can accurately and reliably "talk to one another." Standards are extremely important in communications where the value of a network is to a large extent determined by the size of the community that can be reached. In addition, the investment required in telecommunications networks is very high, and so network operators are particularly interested in having the choice of buying equipment from multiple, competing suppliers, rather than being committed to buying equipment from a single supplier.

Under the new standards-based environment, a properly designed structured cabling system is based around components or wiring units. Each floor or story of an office building can be viewed as a separate wiring unit. On each floor or story of the building, the various workstations located in individual offices or work locations connect horizontally to a single wiring closet. Each of the individual wiring units (stories of the office building) are connected to each other vertically by backbone cables that form the spine of the building's communications network. Once connected to each other, the structured cabling system serves as a generic host to various applications and, unlike the old cable infrastructure that was designed around specific applications, a structured cabling system permits many applications to take advantage of the universal cabling system. As technological innovations maintain pace with growing consumer demand, networking vendors and specifications committees are figuring out ways to transmit larger quantities of data, voice, and video over copper and fiber-optic cable. As a result, the requirements and performance specifications for the standards are continually being updated.

Anatomy of a Structured Cabling System

The ANSI/TIA/EIA-568-A standard separates the components of a structured cabling system into the following six areas: (i) the building's entrance or the entrance facility, (ii) the building's equipment room, (iii) backbone cabling (vertical connection between wiring units), (iv) telecommunications closet, (v) horizontal cabling, and (vi) work area. The building's entrance facility, as defined by ANSI/TIA/EIA-568-A, specifies the location in the building where the in-building cabling infrastructure connects to the outside world. All external cabling (campus backbone cables that connect various buildings in a campus environment, interbuilding cabling, antennae pathways, and cabling owned by telecommunications providers) enter a building and terminate the external path at a single point within the building. The location of the entrance facility is usually either on the first floor or in the basement of the building and must take into consideration the requirements of the telecommunications services required and other utilities (such as CATV, water, and electrical power). Telecommunications carriers are usually required to terminate within 50 feet of a building entrance. The physical requirements of the interface equipment are defined in ANSI/TIA/EIA-569, the Commercial Building Standard for Telecommunications Pathways. The specifications cover telecommunications closet design and cable pathways.

Past the point of demarcation, the building owner provides the equipment and cabling for the in-building network infrastructure. Accordingly, maintenance and operation of equipment past the demarc is the building owner's responsibility. If the entrance facility of the building shares space with the equipment room,the telephone company may refer to the entrance facility as the demarcation point. Some entrance facilities also house telephone or PBX (private branch exchange) equipment.

The next subsystem of structured cabling defined by ANSI/TIA/EIA-568-A is the equipment room, which is a centralized space specified to house more sophisticated equipment than the entrance facility or the telecommunications closet. Often, telephone equipment or data-networking equipment such as routers, switches, and hubs are located there. Computer equipment may possibly be stored there. Backbone cabling is specified to terminate in the equipment. In smaller organizations, it is desirable to have the equipment room located in the same area as the computer room, which houses network servers and possibly phone equipment.

Any room that houses telecommunications equipment, whether its a telecommunications closet or equipment room, should be physically secure. Many data and voice systems have had security breaches because anyone could walk in off the street and gain physical access to the voice/data network cabling and equipment. Some companies go so far as to put alarm and electronic access systems on their telecommunication closets and equipment rooms.

The third subsystem of structured cabling is called backbone cabling. Backbone cabling is sometimes called vertical cabling, cross-connect cabling, riser cabling, or inter-closet cabling. Backbone cabling is necessary to connect entrance facilities, equipment rooms, and telecommunications closets. Backbone cabling consists of not only the cables that connect the telecommunications closets, equipment rooms, and building entrance but also the cross-connect cables, mechanical terminations, or patch cords used for backbone-to-backbone cross-connection. By way of definition, cross-connect is a facility or location within the cabling system that permits the termination of cable elements and the reconnection of those elements by jumpers, termination blocks, and/or cables to another cabling element (another cable or patch panel). Backbone cabling includes: (i) cabling between equipment rooms and building-entrance facilities, (ii) in a campus environment, cabling between buildings' entrance facilities, and (iii) vertical connections between floors. Care must be taken when running backbone cables to avoid sources of electromagnetic interference or radio-frequency interference.

Backbone pathways provide paths for backbone cabling between the equipment room, telecommunications closets, main-terminal space, and entrance facility. The TIA suggests in ANSI/TIA/EIA-569 that the telecommunications closets be stacked on top of one another from floor to floor so that cables can be routed straight up through a riser. The riser is a vertical shaft used to route cable between two floors. Often, it is nothing more complicated than a hole (core) that is drilled in the floor, allowing cables to pass through. A riser shaft has the potential to act as a chimney because the hole between two floors with cable in it could allow fire to spread from floor to floor through the building cable. To prevent such acceleration of the spread and intensity of a fire, building codes require that riser-rated cable have certain fire-resistant qualities. The riser is firestopped by placing special blocking material in the riser at each penetration of walls or ceilings after the cables have been put in place.

The telecommunications closet is the location within a building where cabling components such as cross-connects and patch panels are located. These rooms are where the horizontal structured cabling originates. Horizontal cabling is terminated in patch panels or termination blocks and then routed through horizontal pathways to reach work areas. The telecommunications closet may also contain networking equipment such as LAN hubs, switches, routers, and repeaters. Backbone cabling equipment rooms terminate in the telecommunications closet.

Horizontal cabling, as specified by ANSI/TIA/EIA-568-A, is the cabling that extends from telecommunications closets to the work area and terminates in telecommunications outlets (information outlets or wall plates.) Horizontal cabling includes the following: (i) cable from the patch panel to the work area, (ii) telecommunications outlets, (iii) cable terminations, (iv) cross-connections (where permitted), and (v) a maximum of one transition point. The horizontal pathways are the paths that the horizontal cable takes between the wiring closet and the work area. The most common place in which the horizontal cable is routed is in the space between the structural ceiling and the false (or drop) ceiling.

Cable installers often install cable directly on the upper portion of a false ceiling. This is a poor installation practice because cable could then also be draped across fluorescent lights, power conduits, and air-conditioning ducts. In addition, the weight of cables could collapse the false ceiling. Some local codes may not permit communications cable to be installed without conduit, hangers, trays, or some other type of pathway. In buildings where the ceiling space is also used as part of the environmental air-handling system, i.e., as an air return, plenum-rated cable must be installed in accordance with Article 800 of NEC. Other common types of horizontal pathways include conduit and trays (or wire-ways). Trays are metal or plastic structures that the cable is laid into when it is installed. The trays can be rigid but can also be flexible (in the case of fiber-optic cable, the flexible tubing is sometimes called the inner duct). Both conduit and trays are designed to keep the cable from resting on top of the false ceiling or being exposed if the ceiling is open.

Other commonly used terms in a structured cabling system include (i) ceiling pathways, which are pathways that allow the cable to be run loosely through the ceiling space, (ii) conduit pathways, which have the cable installed in a metallic or plastic conduit, (iii) tray pathways, which are metal or plastic structures used for horizontal cabling, (iv) sleeves, which are the circular openings that are cut in walls, ceilings, and floors, (v) a slot is the same as a sleeve but rectangular in shape, (vi) a core, which is a circular hole that is cut in a floor or ceiling and is used to access the floor above or below.

Finally, the work area is where the network's activity originates or terminates. The work area is the work station where computers, fax machines, and other telecommunications equipment can be found.

ANSI/TIA/EIA-569-A provides some common design considerations for the entrance facility, equipment room, and telecommunications closets with respect to construction, environmental considerations, and environmental controls:

- The door (without sill) should open outward, slide sideways, or be removable. It should be fitted with a lock and be a minimum of 36 inches (.91 meters) wide by 80 inches (2 meters) high.
- Electrical power should be supplied by a minimum of two dedicated 120V-20A nominal, non-switched, AC-duplex electrical outlets. Each outlet should be on separate branch circuits. The equipment room may have additional electrical requirements based on the telecommunications equipment that will be supported there (such as LAN servers, hubs, PBXs, or UPS systems).
- Sufficient lighting should be provided (500 lx or 50-foot candles). The light switches should be located near the entrance door.
- Grounding should be provided and used per ANSI/TIA/EIA-607 (the Commercial Building Grounding and Bonding Requirements for Tele-

communications Standard) and either the NEC or local code, whichever takes precedence.

- These areas should not have false (drop) ceilings.
- Slots and sleeves that penetrate firewalls or that are used for riser cables should be firestopped per the applicable codes.
- Separation of horizontal and backbone pathways from sources of electromagnetic interference (EMI) must be maintained per NEC Article 800.52.
- Metallic raceways and conduits should be grounded.
- Equip all telecommunications closets, the entrance facility, and the equipment room with electrical surge suppression and a UPS (uninterruptible power supply) that will supply that area with at least 15 minutes of standby AC power in the event of a commercial power failure.
- Equip these areas with standby lighting that will last for at least an hour if the commercial power fails.
- Make sure that these areas are sufficiently separated from sources of EMI such as antennas, medical equipment, elevators, motors, and generators.
- Keep a flashlight or chargeable light in an easy-to-find place in each of these areas in case the commercial power fails and the battery-operated lights run down.
- When security, continuity, or other needs dictate, an alternate entrance facility may need to be provided.
- One wall at a minimum should have $^3/_4$-inch (20mm) A-C plywood.
- It should be a dry area not subject to flooding.
- It should be as close to the actual entrance pathways (where the cables enter the building) as possible. Equipment not relating to the support of the entrance facility should not be installed there.
- Environmental controls must be present to provide HVAC at all times. A temperature range of 64-75 degrees Fahrenheit (or 18-24 degrees Celsius) should be maintained, along with 30-55 percent relative humidity. An air filtering system should be installed to protect against pollution and contaminants such as dust.
- Seismic and vibration precautions should be taken.
- The ceiling should be at least 8.0 feet (2.4 meters) high.
- The entrance area to the equipment room should be large enough to allow delivery of large equipment.
- The room should be above water level to minimize danger of flooding.
- The backbone pathways should terminate in the equipment room.
- In a smaller building, the entrance facility and equipment room may be combined into a single room.

- Each floor of a building should have at least one telecommunications closet, depending on the distance to the work areas. The closets should be close enough to the areas being served so the horizontal cable does not exceed a maximum of 90 meters.
- Environmental controls are required to maintain a temperature that is the same as adjacent office areas. Positive pressure should be maintained in the telecommunications closets, with a minimum of one air change per hour (or per local code).

CHAPTER 5

Liability, Indemnification and Insurance

Emergency Access and Entry

Although the building owner should attempt to limit access to the building unless they receive notification from the vendor, the vendor may not be able to provide the proper notification. The vendor should specify terms that allow such emergency access. In times of an emergency, it may also be necessary for the building owner to enter the space and pathways used by the vendor. Such access should be allowable.

Building Codes

Cabling design standards also must satisfy fire-safety requirements imposed by the U.S. National Electrical Code (NEC). The NEC defines levels of cabling and rates them on their flammability, heat resistance, and their ability to generate visible smoke in the event of a fire. In negotiating design specifications for the cabling infrastructure, telecommunications companies and building owners typically battle over whether plenum-rated cables should be used in the building's cable installation. The NEC rates plenum-rated cable as the highest rated cable because of its fire-resistant and low smoke-producing characteristics. In a plenum-rated cable, fluorinated ethylene-propylene is commonly used as conductor insulation, whereas category 5 and non-plenum cables use high-density polyethylene as conductor insulation. Fluorinated ethylene-propylene is more expensive, has better transmission properties, and generates less visible smoke than high-density polyethylene, and as a result, plenum-rated cables are very expensive to install. For both safety and quality reasons, building owners should insist on plenum-rated cables. Building owners should not be surprised, however, if telecommunications companies challenge the requirement of plenum-rated cables. Plenum-rated cables are not only cost prohibitive for the telecommunications company, they may not be required by the fire code or by industry standards in certain non-plenum spaces, and unless specifically required to do so, telecommunication companies will install nonplenum-rated cables in such areas.

Liability

In the context of a telecommunications access agreement, the building owner and the telecommunications service provider have a symbiotic relationship in that both serve the building's tenants. As a provider of broadband services to the building's tenants, the telecommunications company is neither a space tenant nor the building owner's service provider. The building owner merely allows the service provider to access the building in order to create a leasing amenity for the building's tenants. Because the telecommunications company, not the building owner, provides the telecommunications services to the building occupants, it is important to clarify the respective roles of each party to ensure that neither party becomes responsible for unexpected obligations.

Indemnification

The building owner and the vendor should each agree to indemnify and hold each other harmless from and against any claims, damages, costs and expenses arising from negligence unless such liability results from the gross negligence or willful misconduct of either party. The agreement should contain language shielding the vendor from liability for consequential, punitive or special damages, except those incurred through the vendor's gross negligence or willful misconduct. It should also be stated that any of these provisions will survive the expiration or earlier termination of the access agreement.

Most of the form access agreements generally contain detailed provisions pursuant to which each party agrees to indemnify the other for any breach of its representations, warranties, or non-compliance with its covenants or other agreements. While the building owner may be expected to deliver reciprocal indemnification provisions, if the language is limited to indemnification of claims arising from the breach of the buildings owner's representations and warranties, the limited extent of such representations and warranties is such that these provisions are generally not of great concern from a building owner's perspective. The contractual indemnities favoring the building owner, on the other hand, are among the most important and complex components of the access agreement for the building owner. From both a building owner's and a telecommunications company's perspective, express contractual indemnification rights should be specified for several reasons.

Among other things, the contractual indemnification language may expand the parties entitled to seek indemnification by including the indemnitee party's affiliates, officers, directors, shareholders, etc. Additionally, the indemnification language typically expands the scope of recoverable losses by including such costs as attorneys' fees, which are not generally recoverable in litigation as a matter of right. The following building owner-oriented provision deals with indemnification and waiver issues:

Indemnification and Waivers.

(a) <u>Definitions</u>. The "Company Parties" are Company and any Affiliate and their respective owners, directors, officers, managers, employees, agents, and contractors. The "Owner Parties" are Owner, any Affiliate, any holder of a deed of trust or mortgage against the Premises, Premises' telecom manager, and their respective owners, directors, officers, managers, employees, agents or contractors. "Claims" means all claims, demands, proceedings, liabilities, expenses (including reasonable attorneys' and experts' fees), damages, fines and penalties. "Indemnify" means to protect another party against Claims and/or to compensate another party for a Claim incurred. "Defend" means to oppose on behalf of another party a Claim in litigation or other proceeding with counsel satisfactory to the party being defended and to pay all costs associated with the preparation or prosecution of such defense. "Waive" means to relinquish a right or release another party from liability in connection with a Claim. The terms "bodily injury," "property damage" and "personal injury" will have the same definitions as in Insurance Services Office, Inc. ("ISO") form CG 0001 0196, without application of any exclusions contained in such form or in any available endorsement.

(b) <u>Allocation of Risks</u>. Company Waives, and will Indemnify and Defend the Owner Parties against, all Claims arising, or alleged to arise, from the following:

(i) any personal or bodily injury to or suffered by any person which (A) occurs in a portion of the Telecom Space under the exclusive control of Company, whether or not caused by a Company Party, or (B) occurs outside the portion of the Telecom Space under the exclusive control of Company and to the extent caused by a Company Party;

(ii) any personal injury or bodily injury suffered by a Company Party that occurs anywhere in the Premises and to the extent caused by a person other than a Owner Party;

(iii) any property damage (A) to the Premises of a Company Party no matter where the loss occurred or the cause of such loss, or (B) to the Premises of any person other than a Company Party that (1) occurs in any portion of the Telecom Space under the exclusive control of Company, whether or not caused by a Company Party, or (2) occurs outside a portion of the Telecom Space under the exclusive control of Company and to the extent caused by a Company Party;

(iv) any interruption to the business of Company or Claim for loss of use of the Telecom Space or any System suffered by Company; or

(v) any interruption of or defect in the services performed by Company for a resident.

(c) Scope of Indemnities and Waivers. THE INDEMNITIES, WAIVERS AND OBLIGATIONS TO DEFEND CONTAINED IN THIS AGREEMENT SHALL BE ENFORCED FOR THE BENEFIT OF THE BENEFICIARY THEREOF EVEN IF THE CLAIM IN QUESTION IS CAUSED BY THE SOLE, JOINT, CONCURRENT, OR COMPARATIVE NEGLIGENCE OF THE BENEFICIARY THEREOF, AND/OR STRICT LIABILITY IS IMPOSED OR ALLEGED AGAINST THE BENEFICIARY THEREOF, BUT NOT TO THE EXTENT THAT A COURT OF COMPETENT JURISDICTION HOLDS IN A FINAL JUDGMENT THAT A CLAIM IS CAUSED BY THE WILLFUL MISCONDUCT OR GROSS NEGLIGENCE OF SUCH BENEFICIARY.

(d) Survival. The Indemnities, Waivers and obligations to Defend contained in this Agreement are independent of, and will not be limited by, each other or any insurance obligations contained in this Agreement and will survive the expiration or earlier termination of this Agreement until all Claims against Owner Parties are fully and finally barred by applicable statutes of limitations.

Most agreements also contain a provision that exculpates the building owner from all liability, including liability for the building owner's negligence, unless it results from the owner's gross negligence or willful misconduct. While a telecommunications company will not be successful in removing such exculpatory clauses from the agreement, it should negotiate at least a carve-out for liability resulting from the landlord's gross negligence or willful misconduct. In addition to the exculpation clause, the agreement may contain express provisions that waive either party's right to recover consequential or actual damages under the agreement. Lastly, even if the agreement does not allow the building owner to fully exculpate itself from all liability or does not contain blanket waivers of either party's rights to recover damages, the agreement will most likely contain a "non-recourse" provision that limits the building owner's liability to its equity in the property.

Assuming there are no exceptions to the non-recourse provision, a telecommunications company's ability to enforce its remedies through a suit for damages will be futile if the building is highly leveraged by mortgage financing. In determining the potential likelihood of success in filing a suit for damages, a telecommunications company's counsel must evaluate not only the provisions that enable the company to enforce its remedies but also those provisions that castrate the company's ability to realize actual damages if the company is ultimately successful in enforcing its remedies. Finally, while most building owners will not agree to a similar cap on liability in favor of the telecommunications company, the company should insist on a liability cap in certain contexts that could pose unlimited liability, e.g., liabilities arising out of environmental claims. A sample provision limiting the telecommunications company's exposure to liability from consequential damages follows:

> Limitation of Liability. THE COMPANY SHALL NOT BE LIABLE TO [INSERT NAME OF OWNER] FOR ANY LOST PROFITS, SPECIAL, INCIDENTAL, PUNITIVE, EXEMPLARY OR CONSEQUENTIAL DAMAGES, INCLUDING BUT NOT LIMITED TO FRUSTRATION OF ECONOMIC OR BUSINESS EXPECTATIONS, LOSS OF PROFITS, LOSS OF CAPITAL, COST OF SUBSTITUTE PRODUCT(S), FACILITIES OR SERVICES, OR DOWN TIME COST, EVEN IF ADVISED OF THE POSSIBILITY OF SUCH DAMAGES.

Provisions addressing the building owner's interests state:

> Owner's liability for failure to perform its obligations under this Agreement will be recoverable solely out of proceeds from judicial sale upon execution and levy made against Owner's interest in the Premises. Except as provided in the preceding sentence, Company waives (A) all other rights of recovery against any Owner Party, and (B) all Claims against any Owner Party for consequential, special or punitive damages allegedly suffered by any Company Party, including lost profits and business interruption. No Owner Party will have any personal liability under this Agreement.

Owner shall not be liable or responsible to Company for any of the following (collectively, "Equipment Malfunction"): (a) interruption or suspension of electrical service to the System, (b) malfunction or non-functioning of the System, or (c) repair, maintenance or loss of or damage to the System.

Company shall be responsible for providing Company's own backup power supply and power surge protection. Company Waives all Claims against Owner Parties arising, or alleged to arise, from any Equipment Malfunction. Company shall Indemnify and Defend Owner against any Claim made by a customer of Company's Services for any damages whatsoever incurred by the customer which arise, or are alleged to arise, out of any interruption of or defect in Company's Services or any Equipment Malfunction.

Subscription Agreement Provisions

Another way to shield the building owner from liability is to require the vendor to indemnify the owner against claims from the building tenant in the subscription agreement. In each subscription agreement with a building tenant, vendors should be obligated to inform the tenant that the building owner is not a service provider under the agreement, is not related to the vendor in any way, and is not responsible or liable to the tenant for the maintenance, failure, or quality of any communications service received from the vendor. This indemnification should only be related to the services provided by the vendor to the building tenant as detailed in the subscription agreement.

Environmental Concerns and Indemnification

The installation of the in-building infrastructure carries the potential risk that the construction work could trigger environmental concerns. The telecommunications company should require the building owner to disclose the presence of asbestos or any other environmental condition that the building owner becomes aware of during the term of the agreement. Preferably, the building owner should be required to identify the precise location of the environmental condition or the asbestos within the building so that the telecommunications company can avoid exposure to such environmental concerns. From a building owner's standpoint, the building owner should require the telecommunications company to follow specific procedures if the telecommunications company encounters asbestos or any other hazardous materials during its construction work. Additionally, the building owner should impose certain restrictions on the telecommunications company to ensure that the company does not introduce or disturb any hazardous conditions in the building. A sample provision addressing such environmental concerns follows:

- Hazardous Materials. Licensee shall not cause or permit the storage, use, generation or disposition of any Hazardous Materials in the Telecom Space without the prior written consent of Licensor except for the use and storage of supplies used in the ordinary course of Licensee's business (including backup batteries) and then only if (i) such materials are in small quantities, properly labeled and contained, (ii) such materials are used, transported, handled, and disposed of in accordance with the more stringent of Applicable Law or the highest industry standards, and (iii) notice of and a copy of the current national safety data sheet is provided to Licensor for each such hazardous or toxic material. For purposes of this Agreement, the term "Hazardous Materials" means any explosives, radioactive materials or other hazardous substances that are regulated or governed by Applicable Law.

• Existing ACMs and PACMs.

(i) ACM Study. Prior to installing any Telecom Equipment, Licensee shall review the written conclusions of the most recent investigation ("ACM Study"), if any, performed to determine the existence and location of asbestos-containing materials ("ACMs") or presumed asbestos-containing materials ("PACMs") for the portion of the Property in which the Telecom Equipment is to be installed. Licensor shall make the ACM Study available in the Property management office. IN NO EVENT SHALL LICENSEE BEGIN PREPARATION OF INSTALLATION PLANS UNTIL LICENSEE HAS REVIEWED AN ACM STUDY FOR THE PORTION OF THE PROPERTY IN WHICH THE TELECOM EQUIPMENT IS TO BE INSTALLED.

(ii) Compliance. Licensee shall be solely responsible for (A) determining prior to preparation of the Installation Plans with respect to either the initial installation of Telecom Equipment or subsequent connection of any customer to the Telecom Equipment whether any ACMs or PACMs might be disturbed by Licensee's employees or contractors during the installation or connection process, and (B) complying with all Applicable Law, including without limitation giving notices to employees and using contractors certified to work in areas containing ACMs or PACMs. Any required reporting to or contact with any government agency having jurisdiction over the ACMs will be handled by or at the direction of Licensor. IN NO EVENT WILL LICENSEE DISTURB EXISTING ACMS OR PACMS SHOWN IN AN ACM STUDY OR OF WHICH LICENSEE IS AWARE.

(iii) Potential Disturbance of ACMs. If after reviewing an ACM Study for the portion of the Property in which the Telecom Equipment is to be installed, Licensee determines that its installation of the Telecom Equipment might disturb existing ACMs or PACMs, Licensee shall immediately report the potential disturbance to Licensor in writing. If during installation Licensee encounters ACMs or PACMs not shown in an ACM Study, Licensee shall immediately stop work in the affected area, report the condition to Licensor in writing and not resume work in the affected area unless Licensee receives written approval from Licensor. In either such event Licensor shall have the option, exercisable by written notice delivered to Licensee to (A) require that the Telecom Equipment be installed in a portion of the Property where no disturbance of ACMs or PACMs will be necessary, (B) agree to promptly remove, encapsulate or otherwise remediate, at the sole cost of Licensee, the ACMs or PACMs in the portion of the Property in which the Telecom Equipment will be installed, or (C) terminate this Agreement. If Licensor elects either option (A) or (B) set forth in the preceding sentence, Licensee shall have the option to terminate this Agreement exercisable by written notice delivered to Licensor within thirty (30) days after receipt by Licensee of written notice of Licensor's election. If an ACM Study is made available to Licensee, Licensee shall adhere to Licensor's operations and management plan ("O&M Plan") with respect to any work that may involve disturbing any ACMs or PACMs.

- Indemnity. Licensee shall Indemnify and Defend the Licensor Parties against all Claims arising, or alleged to arise, out of (i) any deposit, spill, discharge or other release of Hazardous Materials that occurs in or from the Property as a result of Licensee's operations, (ii) disturbance by a Licensee Party of any ACMs or PACMs, or (iii) Licensee's failure to follow Licensor's O&M Plan.

If any hazardous or toxic substances exist in the building or are introduced to the building by anyone other than the vendor during the term of the agreement, the vendor should have no obligation to remediate, abate or remove any such hazardous or toxic substances, provided that the vendor was not responsible for the presence of such hazardous or toxic substances. In this case, the building owner should indemnify the vendor for any liability, cost, or expense incurred with respect to such hazardous or toxic substances that the vendor has not brought into the building or disturbed in the building.

However, the vendor should indemnify the building owner for any liability, cost, or expense incurred by the owner connected to any such hazardous or toxic substances that the vendor has brought into the building or disturbed in the Building. If the owner becomes aware of the presence or precise location of any hazardous or toxic substances, including, but not limited to, asbestos, that are likely to affect the vendor's operations, the owner should be obligated to promptly notify the vendor in writing of the presence and precise location of such substances. The vendor then should retain the right to immediately terminate the access agreement.

It is a good idea to specify possible types of environmental hazards and liabilities. For example:

For purposes of this Section: (i) "Environmental Hazard" shall mean Hazardous Materials (as defined hereinafter), or the storage, handling, production, disposal, treatment or release thereof; (ii) "Hazardous Material" shall mean (A) any hazardous waste or regulated substance, as defined in the Resource Conversation and Recovery Act (42 U.S.C. § 6901 et seq.); (B) any extremely hazardous substance as defined in the Emergency Planning and Community Right-to-Know Act (42 U.S.C. § 11001 et seq.); (C) any hazardous substances as defined in the Comprehensive Environmental Response, Compensation and Liability Act (42 U.S.C. § 9601 et seq.); (D) any toxic substances as defined in the Toxic Substances Control Act (15 U.S.C. § 2601 et seq.); (E) any pollutant as defined in the Clean Water Act (33 U.S.C. § 1251 et seq.); (F) gasoline, petroleum or other hydrocarbon products or by-products; (G) asbestos or polychlorinated biphenyls; or (H) any other materials, substances, or wastes subject to environmental regulation under any applicable federal, state or local law, regulations, or ordinance now or hereafter in effect; (iii) "Environmental Liabilities" shall mean any liability, penalties, fines, forfeitures, demands, damages, losses, claims, causes of action, suits, judgments, and costs and expenses incidental thereto (including cost of defense, settlement, reasonable attorneys' fees, reasonable consultant fees, and reasonable expert fees), arising from or based on (A) environmental contamination or the threat of environmental contamination or (B) non-compliance with, or violation of, any environmental law or regulation, and shall include, but not be limited to, liability arising from: (1) any governmental action, order, directive, administrative proceeding, or ruling, (2) personal or bodily injuries (including death) or damages to any property (including loss of use) or natural resources, or (3) cleanup, remediation, investigation, monitoring, or other response action.

Insurance

Insurance Rating

The access agreement should prohibit the vendor from engaging in any activity or using equipment in such a way that will cause an increase in the rate of fire or other insurance on the building. If such an increase does occur because of any action of the vendor, the vendor will be required to pay the amount of the increase to the building owner. A period of time should be specified for the vendor to pay the building owner after the owner requests payment. Documentation from an insurance company should be used as evidence of the increase if it states that any action of the vendor led to the increase.

Upon receipt of any such statement, the vendor should reserve the right to challenge the increase or to clarify with the insurer what exactly caused the increase, in order to permit the vendor to attempt to remedy the situation and hopefully reduce or eliminate such additional cost.

Liability and Umbrella Insurance

The vendor should be obligated to, at its sole cost and expense, procure and maintain throughout the term of the access agreement a commercial general liability policy insuring against claims, demands or actions for bodily injury, death, personal injury, and loss or damage to property arising from:

- The condition of or use of the vendor's equipment, the equipment space or the building communications spaces;
- Operations in or maintenance of the vendor's equipment, the equipment space or the building communications spaces;
- The vendor's contractual liability assumed under the access agreement.

Such insurance, together with any umbrella liability insurance, should have a combined single limit as reasonably required by the owner from time to time and have a minimum amount that must be maintained. Endorsements should be obtained for cross-liability, construction, and contractual liability.

The agreement should require the vendor, prior to commencing any work in the building, to provide to the building owner:

- Endorsements to any liability policies, including those of any subcontractors, that name the building owner as an additional insured.
- Certificates of insurance or copies of such insurance policies.

The building owner and vendor can waive any claims each might otherwise have against the other for property damage, even if caused by negligence, if such damage is covered by any policy of insurance.

Any type of insurance or any increase of its limits of liability required by and for the protection of the vendor should be the vendor's own responsibility and should be paid for by the vendor.

Insurance for Personal Property

The vendor should, at its sole cost and expense, procure and maintain throughout the term of the agreement a property insurance policy insuring all of the vendor's personal property located at the site, including but not limited to the communications equipment, for not less than the full replacement cost of said property. All proceeds of such insurance should be used to repair or replace the vendor's property and equipment.

Requirements of Insurance Coverage

All such insurance required to be carried by the vendor should be with an insurance company licensed to do business in the state in which the building is located. The insurance company should also have a Best's Ratings of A or better and a Best's Financial Size Categories of VIII or better and/or Standard & Poor Insurance Solvency Review A- or better. The insurance should also:

- Contain an endorsement that the policy will remain in full force and effect even if the insured releases its right of action against any party before the occurrence of a loss.
- Name the building owner or the owner's property manager and any other party having an interest in the Building as additional insured parties.
- Provide that the policy shall not be cancelled, failed to be renewed, or materially amended without at least thirty (30) days' prior written notice to all parties having an interest in the Building.
- Grant the building owner the right to increase the limits of any insurance required. The agreement should specify the conditions and time periods when such increases can be instituted.

Waiver of Subrogation

Each party should be permitted a waiver of subrogation clause included in the policies as long as such a waiver does not impair the effectiveness of the policy or the insured's ability to recover losses under the policy.

Security System

If the building owner uses a professional security system, access control system, or similar system for the building, it should be understood that such engagement will not increase the owner's liability for occurrences and/or consequences that such a system is designed to detect or avert and that the vendor relies on its insurer for any claims for damages or injury to any person or property.

Notice of Damage

The agreement should require the vendor to notify the building owner promptly of any damage to the building, the equipment space, the building communications spaces or any property or equipment belonging to the owner or any other occupant of the building caused by the vendor. The vendor should agree to be responsible for the payment for any repairs due to any such damage it caused, unless covered and paid for by the insurance coverage.

The liability assumed by the telecommunications company under the indemnification provisions may be and often is transferred to an insurance carrier by means of contractual liability coverage. The advantage of requiring adequate insurance coverage is that it reduces risk and provides additional security against the possibility of loss. The insurance policy may be designed to cover direct or consequential losses, although most policies cover only direct losses, and consequential losses must be insured by a special endorsement or policy. A sample insurance provision follows:

Shielding the Building Owner from Liability

Prior to the delivery of telecommunications services to building tenants, the building owner should require the telecommunications company to communicate to such tenants, and such tenants should acknowledge in writing, that: (i) the telecommunications equipment and services are being provided and maintained by the telecommunications company and not the building owner, (ii) the building owner has no responsibility or liability for the installation, operation, maintenance, use, repair or replacement of the telecommunications equipment, or the provision, quality or sufficiency of the telecommunications services, and (iii) by subscribing to and accepting the telecommunications services, the tenants agree to release the building owner from any such liability.

This is especially important because a broadband network is vulnerable to technical difficulties, network downtime, or other disruptive problems that could interfere with the delivery of communications services to building tenants. Any number of possibilities could cause these service interruptions, including negligence, intentional sabotage, or unanticipated casualty or disaster. For example, the telecommunications company may rely on contractual arrangements with a third party supplier or vendor to provide installation service or equipment for its broadband network within the building. Contractual or other unanticipated service problems or any delays or related problems with delivery of such equipment for the service provider's network buildout can disrupt the delivery of communications services. A natural disaster or other unanticipated interruption of services or damage to the in-building broadband network could also cause service failures. Moreover, unauthorized parties or computer viruses may circumvent even the strictest network security measures and cause disruptions to the delivery of broadband services. Finally, the service provider might inadvertently, or even intentionally, interrupt service while performing routine maintenance or while eliminating breaches of network security.

Building tenants, of course, could incur substantial losses from such failed broadband infrastructure and the resulting service interruptions and network downtime. Too many service interruptions may, in time, damage the building owner's reputation, even though the service provider, not the building owner, is responsible for the delivery of broadband services to tenants. One of the key components of the access agreement, therefore, should be to impose minimum network performance standards that the service provider must maintain during the term of the access agreement. The agreement should require the service provider to invest in state-of-the-art corporate firewall and e-security technologies to prevent any infrastructure failures. Additionally, in order to minimize loss and to ensure continuity of the critical business functions of building tenants in the event of a service failure, the agreement should require the service provider to install back-up equipment and implement, in advance, adequate disaster and business recovery procedures. More importantly, the agreement should obligate the service provider to take immediate action to restore service to building tenants within a reasonable time in the event of a service disruption. The various disaster recovery steps that the service provider might execute should be based on the nature and the magnitude of the service disruption. A sample provision imposing such obligations on the service provider states:

> Licensee shall respond to any problems, complaints, or difficulties asserted by any Tenant with respect to any of the Services provided to such Tenant as follows: (i) within one (1) hour if in response to a major problem, complaint or difficulty, where "major" problems, complaints, and difficulties include, for example, problems that cause any complete or material outage of failure of a Service provided to a Tenant; (ii) within three (3) hours if in response to a minor problem, complaint or difficulty, where "minor" problems, complaints and difficulties include, for example, problems that limit the availability or functionality of a Service provided to a Tenant in any non-material way; and (iii) within twenty-four (24) hours if in response to a purchase order signed by such Tenant for any "moves, adds or changes" (as such terms are customarily used in the communications industry).

In addition to protecting the building owner's reputation, the agreement should shield the building owner against potential liability to, or at least complaints from, the building tenants with respect to broadband service interruptions. While the service contract between the telecommunications company and the building tenant may limit the telecommunications company's liability to the tenant for service disruptions, the building owner may not enjoy similar protections. While the latest space leases between building owners and tenants may address liability issues relating to broadband service failures, the older forms might not have addressed these issues. As a result, a tenant might assert liability against building owners for tenant losses, such as loss of revenues, that are attributable to broadband service disruptions. In order to protect against such claims, whether ultimately valid or not, the access agreement must contain strong indemnification provisions that hold the building owner harmless against claims arising from any loss or damage incurred by the building's tenants due to the delivery of broadband services. The agreement should also clarify the respective roles of the parties and impose obligations on the service provider to ensure that such liability issues do not occur in the first place. The following provisions address these issues:

> Licensor and Licensee acknowledge and agree that the relationship between them is solely that of independent contractors, and nothing shall be construed to constitute as employer and employee, partners, joint venturers, co-owners or otherwise as participants in a joint or common undertaking. Neither party, nor its employees, agents or representatives shall have any right, power, or authority to act or create any obligation, express or implied, on behalf of the other party.
>
> Nothing herein expressed or implied is intended to confer on any person, other than the parties hereto or their respective permitted assigns, successors, heirs, and legal representatives any rights, remedies, obligations or liabilities under or by reason of this Agreement.

Upon commencement of any services to a Tenant, Licensee shall communicate to such Tenant and such Tenant shall acknowledge in writing in effect that (i) the Telecommunications Equipment and the Services are being provided and maintained by Licensee and not Licensor, (ii) Licensor has no responsibility or liability for the installation, operation, maintenance, use, repair, or replacement of the Telecommunications Equipment, or the provision, quality, or sufficiency of the Services, (iii) by subscribing to and accepting the Services, Tenant agrees to release Licensor from any such liability, and (iv) any cessation or interruption in the provision of Services by Licensee does not constitute a default or constructive eviction by Licensor under the property lease between Tenant and Licensor.

CHAPTER 6

Outsourcing of Telecom Operations

In recent years, outsourcing has gained popularity among real estate owners. The ever increasing pace of technological innovation and certain high profile bankruptcies in the telecommunications sector, coupled with the ability to achieve economies of scale through an outsourcing vendor, has spawned a new breed of real estate owners who appreciate the virtues of outsourcing management functions of information technology to vendor companies. By outsourcing, building owners recruit much needed skill and expertise in the management of networks and other telecommunications functions of their buildings because the vendor company serves as an interface between the building owner and the various technology service providers who service the building and its tenants.

In a typical scenario in which a building's technology functions are outsourced, the vendor provides various procurement services that include, among other things, identifying technology service providers with the most favorable terms, acquiring broadband transmission services on behalf of the owner or building tenants, and purchasing equipment, hardware, and software as part of a turnkey project. As part of the administration and management services, the vendor manages, administers, and maintains the various technology agreements retained by the building owner for broadband and other IT-related services. The vendor provides the building owner with reasonable notice of any renewal, termination, or cancellation dates and fees in respect of the broadband and IT services. As technology evolves and new standards for broadband services are set, the vendor evaluates and makes appropriate recommendations to the building owners. If structured properly, the outsourcing agreement will require vendor's project manager and building's management team to meet on regular occasion to review technology evolutions so that significant changes in technology are dealt with and handled in a timely fashion.

Structuring the outsourcing agreement between the building owner and the vendor in a manner that clearly defines the respective rights, expectations, and obligations is crucial. At the outset, it is important to define the baseline of services that the vendor will provide for the building. To the extent the building owner wants to purchase additional services above the baseline, the outsourcing agreement should contain appropriate carve-outs. Equally important is the allocation of responsibility over third-party leases and maintenance agreements respecting broadband services and hardware equipment and machines. Among other things, the agreement should allocate responsibilities for: (i) maintaining, upgrading, and providing management services for the broadband transmission media and equipment, (ii) monitoring compliance of hardware leases and third-party technology agreements serving the building, (iii) retaining financial and administrative responsibility for applications and systems software, (iv) defining business and technical requirements for the building, (v) procuring future LAN/server equipment, software, cabling/wiring, (vi) managing network design and project planning, (vii) troubleshooting/resolving interference with services, (viii) managing riser capacity and network needs for building tenants, and (ix) monitoring and managing networks providing voice and data needs for the building.

Specifying the performance standards governing the vendor's provision of services is also important. The agreement should define a benchmark for acceptable performance standards and specify liquidated damages if the vendor fails to perform in accordance with such performance standards. As the interface between the building owner and the technology service providers, the vendor and its employee will transact on behalf of the building owner. For this reason, the building owner should ensure that the vendor's employment screening procedures are consistent with the building owner's policies and procedures. The building's management team, vendor's project manager, and certain key employees who will service the building should be identified in the agreement. The owner might consider restricting the vendor from authorizing any employee who is not listed in the agreement to transact on behalf of the building owner. Additionally, for security reasons, the building owner should limit the number of vendor employees who will have access to the building and its tenants. Procedures pursuant to which the building owner reviews, approves, and grants request for access for both routine and emergency reasons by privileged vendor employees should be in place.

As with any relationship, planning for exit strategies in the event the relationship fails to yield the expected returns is also important. The agreement should contain clauses that allow the building owner certain termination rights that might include, depending on the circumstances and negotiations leverage, termination for convenience, termination upon change of control of building owner, termination upon change of control of vendor, termination for breach of outsourcing contract, termination for failure to provide critical service, and termination for substantial changes in business of either building owner or vendor. The termination fees, if any, should be specified, and the respective rights and obligations upon termination should be addressed. In addition to addressing termination rights and fees, if appropriate, the agreement should contain a plan to transition the outsourced services from the vendor to its successor. The agreement should also contain provisions dealing with any particular building operations that might be affected by the transition. For example, are there any operations that can not be down for more than a limited amount of time? If so, will there be a cut-off procedure in place to deal with these operations as the outsourcing agreement is transitioned to a different vendor?

Here are some definitions and suggested provisions that might be used in the outsourcing agreement, assuming the final business discussions require their use:

Suggested Provisions for Outsourcing Agreement

(a) <u>Definitions</u>

The following defined terms shall have the meanings specified below:

"Owner Data" shall mean all data and information submitted to Vendor by Owner in connection with the Services.

"Owner Machines" shall mean those machines and equipment owned or leased by Owner, including those machines and equipment set forth in the attached Exhibit.

"Owner Project Executive" shall mean the individual who is appointed by Owner who will act as the primary point of contact for Vendor with respect to each party's obligations under this Agreement.

"Owner Proprietary Software" shall mean the software owned by Owner set forth in Exhibit ___, as may be updated from time to time during the Term.

"Owner Service Locations" shall mean the service locations owned, leased, or under the control of Owner that are set forth in Exhibit ___.

"Owner Software" shall mean the Owner Proprietary Software, the Owner Third Party Software, and any related documentation in Owner's possession on or after the Effective Date.

"Owner Third Party Software" shall mean the software licensed or leased by Owner from a third party which is set forth in Exhibit ___, as may be updated from time to time during the Term.

"Developed Software" shall mean (a) any modifications or enhancements to the Owner Software and (b) any software and related documentation developed pursuant to this Agreement by Vendor, its subcontractors or agents.

"Disaster" shall mean the occurrence of a disaster at a Service Location as that term is commonly referred to in the telecommunication industry at that time.

"Force Majeure Event" shall mean any failure or delay caused, directly or indirectly, by fire, flood, earthquake, elements of nature or acts of God, acts of war, terrorism, riots, civil disorders, rebellions or revolutions in the United States, strikes, lockouts or labor difficulties, court order, third-party nonperformance (except the non-performing party's subcontractors or agents), or any other similar cause beyond the reasonable control of such party and without the fault or negligence of such party.

"Key Employee(s)" shall mean the Project Staff members who are (a) assigned to the key positions identified in Exhibit ___ and (b) identified, and agreed upon, by the Owner Project Executive and the Vendor Project Executive as important to a particular Project.

"Termination Assistance Services" shall mean (1) the cooperation of Vendor with Owner in effecting the orderly transfer of the Services to a third party or the resumption of the Services by Owner upon request by Owner and (2) the performance by Vendor of such services as may be requested by Owner in accordance with Exhibit ___, in connection with the transfer of the Services to a third party or the resumption of the Services by Owner.

"Vendor Machines" shall mean those machines and equipment owned or leased by Vendor, including those machines and equipment set forth in Exhibit ___.

"Vendor Proprietary Software" shall mean the software and related documentation (a) owned by Vendor prior to the Effective Date which is used in connection with the Services or (b) of which Vendor acquires ownership after the Effective Date, or is developed by or on behalf of Vendor after the Effective Date, and used in connection with the Services that is not Owner Software or Developed Software.

"Vendor Systems" shall mean the Vendor Software and the Vendor Machines, collectively.

(b) Performance Standards

"Base Services." (1) Vendor shall provide the Services at each of the Owner Service Locations at least at the Base Performance Standards for such Owner Service Location described in Exhibit ___.

"Adjustment of Performance Standards." Owner and Vendor shall jointly review during the last quarter of every Year and may adjust, as appropriate, the Performance Standards for the following Year. In addition, either Owner or Vendor may, at any time upon notice to the other party, initiate discussions to review and adjust any Performance Standard which such party in good faith believes is inappropriate at that time.

"Reports." As part of the Base Services, Vendor shall provide monthly performance reports to Owner in a form agreed upon by Owner and Vendor.

"Root-Cause Analysis." After receipt of notice from Owner in respect of Vendor's failure to provide the Services in accordance with the Performance Standards, Vendor shall within [number] days (1) perform a root-cause analysis to identify the cause of such failure, (2) correct such failure, (3) provide Owner with a report detailing the cause of, and procedure for correcting, such failure, and (4) provide Owner with reasonable evidence that such failure will not reoccur.

(c) Continued Provision of Services

"Disaster Recovery." As part of the Base Services, Vendor shall (1) assume responsibility for and manage Owner's existing disaster recovery plans as described in Exhibit ___, (2) develop, submit to Owner for its approval and, upon Owner's approval, implement and manage disaster recovery plans for the Service Locations in accordance with Exhibit ___, (3) within [number] days of the Effective Date, and at least once every calendar year during the Term, update and test the operability of the disaster recovery plan in effect at that time, (4) upon Owner's request, certify to Owner that the disaster recovery plans are fully operational, and (5) upon discovery by Vendor, immediately provide Owner with a notice of a Disaster and implement the disaster recovery plans upon the occurrence of a Disaster at a Service Location or otherwise affecting the provision or receipt of the Services.

"Force Majeure." Any failure or delay by Owner or Vendor in the performance of its obligations pursuant to this Agreement shall not be deemed a default of this provided that such failure or delay could not have been prevented by reasonable precautions and cannot reasonably be circumvented by the non-performing party through the use of alternate sources, workaround plans, or other means to the extent such failure or delay is a Force Majeure Event. Upon the occurrence of a Force Majeure Event, the non-performing party shall be excused from any further performance of its obligations pursuant to this Agreement affected by the Force Majeure Event for as long as (1) such Force Majeure Event continues and (2) such party continues to use commercially reasonable efforts to recommence performance whenever and to whatever extent possible without delay. The party delayed by a Force Majeure Event shall immediately notify the other party by telephone (to be confirmed in a notice within [number] days of the inception of such delay) of the occurrence of a Force Majeure Event and describe in reasonable detail the nature of the Force Majeure Event.

"Most Favored Owner." Vendor's charges to Owner for the Services shall be at least as low as Vendor's lowest charges for such services to any of Vendor's similarly situated owners within the _____ industry receiving comparable goods and services at comparable volumes, upon terms and conditions comparable to those contained in this Agreement. Upon Owner's request, Vendor shall advise Owner in writing that this Section ____ has not been contradicted by any transaction entered into by Vendor since the later of (1) the Effective Date or (2) the date of the most recent written notice provided by Vendor pursuant to this Section ____.

(d) Representations and Warranties

Vendor represents and warrants that: (1) it is a corporation duly incorporated, validly existing and in good standing under the laws of _____, (2) it has all requisite corporate power and authority to execute, deliver, and perform its obligations under this Agreement, (3) the execution, delivery and performance of this Agreement have been duly authorized by Vendor, (4) no approval, authorization, or consent of any governmental or regulatory authority is required to be obtained or made by it in order for it to enter into and perform its obligations under this Agreement, (5) in connection with providing the Services, it shall comply with all applicable Federal, state, and local laws and regulations and has obtained all applicable permits, rights, and licenses, (6) the Vendor Proprietary Software does not and will not, and the provision of the Services and the Developed Software (except for any code or materials provided or created by Owner, its subcontractors or agents) will not, infringe upon the proprietary rights of any third party, (7) it has not disclosed as of the Effective Date any Confidential Information relating to Owner, and (8) it is either the owner or authorized by the owner of the machines to use such machines in accordance with the terms of this Agreement.

(e) Termination

"Termination for Convenience." Owner may terminate this Agreement in its entirety at any time upon at least 30 days' written notice to Vendor.

"Termination for Change in Control." In the event of the sale of all or substantially all of the assets of Owner or a merger, corporate reorganization, or change of control of Owner, Owner may terminate this Agreement upon written notice from Owner given within [number] months after the change of control.

In the event of the sale of all or substantially all of the assets of Vendor or a merger, corporate reorganization, or change of control of Vendor, Owner may terminate this Agreement upon [number] days' written notice to Vendor given within [number] months of Owner's receipt of notice of such change of control. Vendor shall promptly notify Owner of the consummation of any of the transactions described in this Section _____.

"Partial Termination." Owner may terminate this Agreement in part with respect to only certain Service Locations at any time during the Term upon [number] days' notice to Vendor.

As part of the Base Services, Vendor shall perform the Termination Assistance Services for up to [number] days prior to the expiration or termination of this Agreement and for up to one year following the expiration or termination of this Agreement.

(f) Exit Plan

Upon the expiration of this Agreement or the termination of this Agreement for any reason:

- Vendor shall provide the Termination Assistance Services in accordance with Article __;
- Owner shall allow Vendor to use, at no charge, those Owner facilities being used to perform the Termination Assistance Services for as long as Vendor is providing the Termination Assistance Services to enable Vendor to effect an orderly transition of Vendor's resources;
- each party shall have the rights specified in Article ____ in respect of the Software;
- upon Owner's request, with respect to Vendor Proprietary Software used to provide the Services as of the date of such expiration or termination, Vendor shall grant to Owner a non-exclusive, royalty-free license to use the Vendor Proprietary Software solely in connection with Owner's business.
- upon Owner's request, with respect to Vendor Third Party Software used to provide the Services as of the date of such expiration or termination, Vendor shall transfer, assign, or sublicense such Vendor Third Party Software to Owner pursuant to Section _____ and pay any transfer fee or non-recurring charge imposed by the applicable Vendor;
- upon Owner's request, with respect to any contracts applicable to services being provided to Owner for maintenance, disaster recovery services, and other necessary third party services being used by Vendor to perform the Services as of the expiration or termination, Vendor (a) shall transfer or assign such agreements to Owner or its designee, on terms and conditions acceptable to both parties, and (b) pay any transfer fee or non-recurring charge imposed by the applicable vendors; and

- upon Owner's request, Vendor shall sell to Owner or its designee the Vendor Machines being used to provide the Services, free and clear of all liens, security interests, or other encumbrances, at the lesser of book and fair market value.

(g) Indemnification

Vendor shall indemnify Owner from, and defend Owner against, any liability or expenses arising out of or relating to (1) any claim by a third party that (a) the Services, (b) the Vendor Proprietary Software, or (c) the Developed Software infringe upon the proprietary rights of any third party, (2) any claim by a third party in respect to services or systems provided by Vendor to a third party, (3) any amounts including taxes, interest, and penalties assessed against Owner that are obligations of Vendor, (5) the inaccuracy or untruthfulness of any representation or warranty made by Vendor under this Agreement, (6) claims arising out of Vendor's breach or violation of Vendor's subcontracting arrangements, (7) (i) a violation of Federal, state, or other laws or regulations for the protection of persons or members of a protected class or category of persons by Vendor or its employees, subcontractors or agents, (ii) sexual discrimination or harassment by Vendor, its employees, subcontractors or agents, (iii) work-related injury except as may be covered by Owner's workers' compensation or death caused by Vendor, its employees, subcontractors, or agents, and (iv) vested employee benefits of any kind expressly assumed by Vendor, (8) relating to inadequacies in the physical and data security control systems at the Service Locations to the extent such systems are controlled or provided by Vendor after the Effective Date, and (9) tangible personal or real property damage resulting from Vendor's acts or omissions. Vendor shall be responsible for any costs and expenses incurred by Owner in connection with the enforcement of this Section ___.

(h) Insurance

"Insurance." During the Term, Vendor shall maintain [, and shall cause its subcontractors to maintain,] at Vendor's own expense insurance of the type and in the amounts specified below:

- errors and omission insurance in the amount of $_____ issued by [insurance company];
- statutory workers compensation in accordance with all Federal, state, and local requirements, employee liability in an amount not less than $_____ per occurrence;
- comprehensive general public liability (including contractual liability insurance) in an amount not less than $_____ [per occurrence]; and

- comprehensive automobile liability covering all vehicles that Vendor owns, hires, or leases in an amount not less than $_____ per occurrence (combined single limit for bodily injury and property damages).

"Documentation." Each such insurance policy shall name Owner as a loss payee and shall provide for at least [number] days' notice to Owner in the event of any modification or cancellation, and in such event, Vendor shall secure replacement insurance to be effective upon expiration or termination of the earlier policy so that there is no lapse in coverage. Vendor will also notify Owner at least [number] days in advance if Vendor desires to materially modify or cancel any such insurance. Upon request, Vendor shall furnish Owner with certificates of insurance to evidence its compliance with the provisions hereof.

(i) Assignment & Change of Control

Neither party may assign this Agreement or any of its rights or obligations hereunder without the consent of the other party and any such attempted assignment shall be void, except that Owner may assign this Agreement or any of its rights or obligations hereunder without the consent of Vendor (a) pursuant to a change of control, including a merger, corporate reorganization, or sale of substantially all of its assets, or (b) to an affiliate. Any assignment in contravention of this Section ___ shall be deemed null and void.

CHAPTER 7

Conclusions

Introduction

The battle for last mile customers has left many casualties in its wake, wiping out most of the entrepreneurial startups that were vying to connect the world to hyperfast, constant Internet access. The handful of survivors who had the agility to change course quickly as the market collapsed around them are now hoarding cash and focusing on increasing revenues from their existing customer base. Despite the much publicized collapse of the broadband revolution, demand for broadband communications remains healthy as businesses increase their reliance on computing and communications technology to compete in today's global business environment. Today, advances in computing and communications technology have advanced so far that they have become indispensable to both individuals and businesses.

In retrospect, the hundreds of startups that sprouted up in search of last mile customers peddled flawed business models. They spent outrageous amounts deploying expensive in-building broadband infrastructure but failed to attract the customers and the revenues necessary to recoup their in-building investments. With the overall venture capital market collapsing around them and facing increased competition from other startups that were also battling for the same universe of customers clustered in metropolitan cities, these companies soon realized that their economic share of the pie would be relatively small and, unfortunately, not enough to justify their expensive build-out strategies. This chapter will review the BLEC's business strategies, identify mistakes made by these BLECs and analyze lessons learned by the telecommunications industry for the future.

BLEC's Business Strategy

With a sizable market comprised of small and medium-sized businesses clustered in the 750,000-plus commercial office buildings scattered throughout the United States, the BLEC industry, in 2000, deployed an aggressive business strategy to reach those businesses and buildings whose network infrastructure lacked a high-speed Internet connection. Most industry experts estimated that in 2000 less than three percent of the multi-tenanted commercial office buildings were connected to a high-speed network. Capitalizing on strong demand for broadband technology by businesses, BLECs positioned themselves as providers of affordable data communications and information technology products. Building owners seeking to stay competitive within the rental marketplace by offering the latest technology amenities to their tenants recognized the need to partner with these BLECs. Building owners and BLECs memorialized these partnerships in long-term license agreements that provided for, among other things, the right of access and entry to the BLECs into the buildings for the installation and maintenance of in-building telecommunications infrastructure and marketing and sales support to help the BLECs penetrate the captive tenants within those buildings.

Through strategic arrangements with the building owners, the various building-centric data services providers developed comprehensive data network solutions that promised to eliminate the bandwidth bottleneck encountered by the building tenants. Hoping to install scaleable, inexpensive, and rapidly deployable proprietary broadband infrastructure throughout the building's riser system, the BLECs aimed to own and operate the critical "last mile" broadband infrastructure. Once the infrastructure was in place, the BLECs expected to develop comprehensive network solutions that, along with high-speed Internet access, bundled content, applications, and e-commerce solutions to generate maximum revenues from buildings, while providing a compelling value proposition to building tenants and enhancing the building owner's competitive market position.

A business strategy depending upon penetration of value-added services to the captive tenant base through the use of high-speed networks, customized web portals, bundled products, and delivery and hosting of applications made sense, of course, only if customer demand within the buildings justified the capital outlay. Carefully balancing the BLEC's initial capital outlay with the projected customer demand for high-speed access and other bundled services became the primary focus, therefore, of pre-wiring due diligence for BLECs. As part of their pre-wiring due diligence, companies deployed engineering and sales teams to the target buildings in advance of contract negotiations with the building owners to assess existing in-building network design and architecture and projected demand among existing tenants for broadband services. In surveying present and future bandwidth requirements of building tenants, companies analyzed the building's square footage, existing bandwidth resources, and broadband infrastructure for the building, and the building's tenant mix. A detailed survey of the building site included identification of horizontal and vertical pathways within the riser system for the installation of network infrastructure and the identification of cabinetry and communications parts within the building. Once the site review and due diligence was complete, the BLECs prepared a detailed network design and architecture construction plans and presented the plans to the building owner for approval. Finally, if the customer demand within the building was strong and the existing broadband infrastructure was lacking, the company then committed to investing capital expenditures to design, install, own, and operate its own communications network for the buildings.

Most companies took this step. In some cases, they deployed Fast Ethernet, engineered to transmit gigabits of data, while in other cases, the companies installed copper or fiber-optic cables in the riser systems of the buildings. The in-building broadband infrastructure, once installed, typically originates at the main distribution frame of the building, terminates on each floor of the building, and extends to the tenant's desktop, once service is ordered by the tenant. The main distribution frame of the building is typically located in the basement or first floor of the building. In the main distribution frame room of the building, telecommunications equipment consisting of switches and routers serve as the aggregator and main transmit point for the building's voice, data, and video traffic entering and exiting the building. The BLECs' in-building infrastructure is typically connected to the local loop network attached to the building and other facilities of Internet service providers.

One of the most economically sound methods of deploying shared services to building tenants was to lease one or multiple T-1 circuits or fiber optic cables and then transport broadband services to multiple tenants within the building. The BLECs utilized a variety of solutions including fiber optic, DSL, and wireless services to provide broadband capability to building tenants. In addition to installing and operating communications infrastructure at no cost to the building owner, some BLECs developed and operated web portals for buildings at no cost. The web portal enabled building owners and tenants to communicate electronically, and most importantly, the web portal contained customized content, services, and applications that were supposed to increase building-specific revenues for the BLEC.

Mistakes Made and Lessons Learned

The BLEC industry exploded onto the marketplace at a time when venture capital money was overflowing, perceived demand for broadband communications was exaggerated, and competition for customers was intense. Companies grew their business rapidly in an attempt to gain first-mover advantage and, as a result, experienced significant losses in their efforts to penetrate the market. Because of the limited operating history of these companies, evaluating the BLEC business model became difficult, and investors, strategic partners, and building owners failed to heed the obvious warning signs until it was too late. To make matters worse, the BLEC model, like the telecommunications industry in general, is capital intensive, evolves rapidly due to both regulatory and technological advances and changes, and requires substantial additional capital to finance its operation in the future. A company's inability to grow rapidly and obtain additional capital, therefore, created a clear disadvantage for some BLECs as they competed with larger and more established companies in the marketplace.

BLECs also faced intense competition from various telecommunications companies, most of whom had significantly greater financial resources and capabilities, were well-established brand names, and had existing customer bases within the commercial office building space. Some of these competitors included local, long distance, cable modem, Internet, digital subscriber line, microwave, mobile, and satellite data service providers. While not all of the competitors focused on the niche market consisting of the underserved small and medium-sized enterprises within commercial office buildings, there were enough competitors vying for the niche customer base in the office buildings that increased competition created intense price wars and impeded the BLEC's ability to become profitable.

In the beginning, BLECs attempted to address in-building competition by structuring exclusive access agreements with building owners and gaining first-mover advantage in penetrating customer base within buildings. The FCC eventually banned exclusive contracts, thus taking away any potential competitive edge that holders of exclusive contracts once possessed. In most buildings, economies of scale were such that multiple in-building service providers could not justify significant capital expenditures required to deploy broadband infrastructure to compete profitably for the target business tenants. BLECs also experienced competitive disadvantages from larger telecommunications companies that had established brand name and reputation with building customers, had significant capital to deploy network architecture rapidly, and had the ability to bundle data and video services with their voice services to achieve economies of scale in servicing existing customers within the buildings.

Substantial price competition within buildings meant that the BLEC business model depended upon the BLEC's ability to install as many in-building networks as possible. The current regulatory environment provides building owners the ability to grant or renew access rights on discretionary terms, thus, creating yet another obstacle for the BLEC in acquiring the needed customer base. The incumbent local exchange carriers ("ILEC"), however, were not burdened by this competitive disadvantage as their legacy access to customers enabled the ILECs to offer bundled services through existing network infrastructure.

In addition to the building owner acting as a potential obstacle to the BLEC's expansion plans, other third parties also served as potential obstacles to the BLECs. For example, the BLECs constructed the in-building broadband infrastructure, but then relied on other communications carriers to provide transmission capacity outside the buildings. The BLEC's inability to obtain adequate connection from other carriers on a timely basis served as an impediment to the BLEC's ability to provide services and generate revenues. In addition, in some markets, redundant connections were either not available or available at cost prohibitive terms, which meant that service interruptions and insufficient transmission capacity would have eventually forced BLECs to lose customers and incur damage to their business reputation. The BLECs also relied on major equipment suppliers, such as Nortel Networks and Cisco Systems, to purchase its in-building broadband equipment. An increase in costs of acquiring this equipment or any shortage of available equipment in the market served as potential obstacles to the BLEC business plans.

Lastly, the BLEC business model depended upon the investment of significant capital expenditure before the generation of revenues, which the BLEC might or might not have recouped. Once the BLEC entered into a telecommunications access agreement with the building owner, the BLEC typically installed an in-building network at its own cost and expense, thus, incurring significant capital expenditures. Depending on the size of the building and any construction-related difficulties that the BLEC may have encountered, these capital expenditures created severe disadvantages for the BLEC. Because the BLEC incurred these capital expenditures before soliciting and obtaining any customers in the building, the BLEC gambled on the probability that it could recoup its expenditures within any building. Adding to the complications, in-building competition for the limited number of potential customers within any building guaranteed failure for the BLEC business model in most cases.

The Changing Face of Government Regulation

The BLECs are subject to numerous local regulations such as building and electrical codes, as well as other laws and regulations applicable to telecommunications companies generally. Changes in the telecommunications regulatory environment affects the BLEC business model by increasing competition, decreasing potential revenue, increasing costs or impairing the BLEC's ability to offer certain services as part of its bundled network solutions. Proposals for regulatory changes applicable to building access and the industry's ability to provide certain telecommunications and Internet services could change from time to time and such changes may have adverse effects on the BLEC's ability to run a profitable business. To make matters worse, a BLEC will never have the ability to predict how regulatory changes will affect their proposed growth plans.

An intense debate over the need for regulating the telecommunications industry has always existed throughout American history. Regulation has evolved from once protecting the rights of a monopoly regime to now creating a competitive environment that values the free entry of entrepreneurs in the telecommunications marketplace. The desirable extent and effect of competition in the telecommunications industry, however, has always been a matter of serious debate. Although most policymakers and corporate players in today's telecommunications environment endorse a competitive marketplace, both groups have universally rejected completely unrestrained competition in the telecommunications industry. The justification of a regulatory regime to protect the interests of both industry players and the consumers that they serve has always been the importance of telecommunications to our nation's economic and social interests. The universal need for access to telecommunications services is now widely recognized, and the significance of telecommunications is obvious from both a macroeconomic and microeconomic point of view.

The argument over the need for regulations to promote competition in the telecommunications market has been a long and continuing one, but the industry, once the leading proponent of such regulation, has since become the leading opponent. The detailed supervision of the telecommunications industry by both federal regulators and local authorities and the powerful controls such governmental bodies possess over all telecommunications companies provide regulation of an intensity paralleled in few other types of economic activity. The significance of telecommunications to individuals, businesses, and economic life, in addition to the technical nature of the industry, are among the justifications for the omnipresent arm of the government. The highly competitive nature of the telecommunications industry and the environment in which it operates has largely precluded a system of self-regulation that would eliminate the need for most governmental supervision.

Articulating the purposes of the thousands of administrative regulations, statutes, and codes that have been imposed on the telecommunications industry in the United States is virtually impossible. Similarly, capturing a one, all-embracing theory of telecommunications regulation is difficult, if not impossible. However, some of the most obvious and overriding aims of the telecommunications codes and regulations pertain to (i) creating a competitive telecommunications market that contributes to the development of innovative technologies that are offered to consumers at competitive prices, (ii) developing minimum safety requirements for constructing, designing and installing cabling systems that protect life, health and property, and (iii) developing cabling specifications and standards to ensure system functionality and to ensure construction quality.

Past and Future

Hoping to reap some of the enormous riches from the lucrative business opportunities created by satisfying the insatiable demand for broadband services among the underserved small and medium-sized businesses, BLECs rushed into access deals with building owners. Vying for access rights to densely populated commercial buildings, most BLECs visualized their business strategy by seeing the forest through the trees. As startups hungered for funding from the robust public markets, BLECs were more focused on their short-term goals of amassing large real estate portfolios than on issues with potential long-term consequences. Accordingly, in the early period of the industry's development, building owners exploited this self-imposed pressure on the BLECs in order to achieve contractual advantage.

Recognizing the prospects for increased revenue by leasing assets previously thought to be of no value, building owners were also eager to enter into access agreements with the BLECs. Eager to fully exploit their buildings' profit potential and yielding to their tenants' demand for bandwidth-intensive, last-mile solutions, these building owners entered into deals without fully understanding all of the complex technical and business issues involved in managing broadband technologies.

The industry, however, has changed. The beleaguered telecommunications industry, faced with global consolidation, and the turbulent stock market have changed the market condition for the surviving, cash-constrained BLECs. As capital becomes more expensive or runs dry for the surviving BLECs, a BLEC-oriented contract is typically structured in a manner that enables the BLEC to deploy its broadband infrastructure in buildings only if the BLEC signs up enough subscribing tenants to help recoup its capital investment.

Competition has reemerged in the last mile space. Consolidation in the industry has enabled the handful of survivors to capture economies of scale and become more competitive. A competitive landscape has also forced companies to spend more resources satisfying customers, increase productivity, and find new opportunities to generate additional revenues through new product offerings. The demand for faster transmission speed and bundled services offering multimedia capability remain the primary drivers for broadband adoption, spurring incremental broadband subscriptions. As a result, technological innovations are likely in the near future.

The transmission media, such as copper, coaxial cable and microwaves, although inexpensive compared to fiber optics, have limited bandwidth capabilities. Fiber-optic cables, however, are expensive to install. These challenges have acted as major inhibitors to ubiquitous deployment of high-speed Internet access. Capital expenditures necessary to deploy broadband solutions to the end users must be contained and, more importantly, operational expenditure must be monitored to assure maximum flexibility in generating increased revenues. Bundled service offerings, technological innovations, and regulatory shifts will raise new issues for lawyers as issues unheard of today will emerge as future materials for the next update to this book.

From a historical perspective, the breakup of the AT&T Bell System in 1984 launched a telecommunications revolution. In the late 1990s, companies that did not exist ten or fifteen years ago challenged Ma Bell's leadership in the telecommunications industry. New companies continued to flow like mountain springs, each hoping to carve a new river in the technology marketplace. During the late 1990s and the early part of 2000, we envisioned an industry that continually spawned new business entrants to address business applications undreamed of today at prices driven down by fierce competition. Notwithstanding the fact that new technologies are being tested and existing technologies are being aggressively deployed, high-speed access to the Internet is not a reality for all users.

The general state of the telecommunications industry today, touching on global consolidation and the turbulent stock market has changed the landscape of the telecommunications industry once again. Today, an oligopoly of telecommunications companies is snapping up, at fire-sale prices, the valuable broadband assets of once high-flying companies, hoping to capture profits by building powerful networks that are capable of satisfying the still-growing demand for broadband services. Hoping to bring the last mile solution to every office building in the United States, the remaining BLECs and the giant telecommunications companies are racing forward at the speed of light, like the bits in fiber, to connect the last end user to the Information Superhighway. The challenge for all parties is to transact in a sufficiently intelligent manner so as to preserve flexibility and adaptability to both the ever changing technology of the industry and the constantly evolving demands of the business community.

The boom and bust cycle of the broadband revolution will continue until the new industry leaders and the preferred technologies gain dominance. Meanwhile, a consolidated telecommunications industry, like the airline industry and the other industries that have transitioned from competition to consolidation in the past, will refocus its financial and technological resources to deliver innovative and inexpensive technologies that address the still-growing needs of today's business community. Although one may be confident that the demand for bandwidth-intensive communications services will grow exponentially in the coming years, which of the remaining broadband companies will remain standing after the recent bear market attack is anybody's guess.

APPENDIX I

Technology Glossary

Amplifier: a device that boosts the signal strength

Analog: voice and visual information transmitted through communications pathways in the form of signals that exactly reproduce the sound or image being transmitted

ANSI/TIA/EIA-568: The Commercial Building Telecommunications Cabling Standard

ANSI/TIA/EIA-569: The Commercial Building Standard for Telecommunications Pathways

ATM: asynchronous transfer mode; blends fast packet switching and multiplexing techniques to create a process of information transfer in the form of fixed length packets

Attenuation: signal level or amplitude loss

Bandwidth: a measure of the amount of data a transmission medium can carry

BLEC: building local exchange carriers; telecommunications companies offering broadband services intended to close the last mile gap. They partner with building owners to offer broadband services to building tenants.

Broadband: networks that transmit data faster than 1.5 Mbps

Circuit Switching: establishes a temporary, dedicated, end-to-end connection between two stations through the nodes of the network

Coaxial Cable: a high capacity cable consisting of an insulated central copper or aluminum conductor surrounded by an outer metallic sheath and an insulating jacket

Digital: uses a binary code to represent information

DS-0: digital signal level zero, the basic building block of the digital network

DSL: digital subscriber line; uses existing phone lines to provide continuous connection to the Internet without causing busy signals

Earth station: receives and transmits microwave transmission from satellites

Fixed Wireless: point-to-point transmission through the air between stationary devices

Frame Relay: a network interface protocol that uses variable-length packets, called frames, to transfer units of data within the network

Frequency division multiplexing (FDM): a form of multiplexing that uses multiple frequencies

Guided Transmission Media: various types of cable; constrain electromagnetic or acoustical waves within boundaries established by their physical construction

LAN: local area network; communications networks within a small geographical space

Modem: device that converts analog data into digital data, allowing computers to communicate over analog phone lines

Multimode Optical Fiber: a type of guided transmission media; concentric cylinders made of dielectric materials; the core houses the glass or plastic strand or fiber in which the lightwave travels. The core is shielded by cladding and a light absorbing jacket; have wider cores than single mode fibers, which allows the electromagnetic wave (lightwave) to enter at various angles, and reflect off core-cladding boundaries as light propagates from transmitter to receiver

Multiplexing: combines and transmits two or more individual signals over the same transmission path

NEC: National Electrical Code

Network Hub: the central connecting component of a network

Node: connection point along a network

Optical Fiber: a cable with a core that houses the glass or plastic strand/fiber through which the lightwave travels. The core is shielded by cladding and a light absorbing jacket.

PAM: pulse amplitude modulation; process by which analog signal is sampled and coverted to pulses; this is part of the PCM process

PCB: a printed circuit board

PCM: pulse code modulation; process that converts an analog signal to a digital signal

PDS: Premises Distribution System; composed of wire, cable, and other equipment necessary to link desktop terminals (workstation locations) with telephone switch, computer, image, video and other information hosts, and with external telecommunications networks

Packet Switching: like the circuit-switched network, this is a collection of nodes interconnected by transmission links over indefinite distances. Unlike the circuit-switched network, a packet-switched network switches and transports signals in a cluster of bits that are switched and transmitted as a single unit called a packet. Because packets are transmitted in bursts as they are received, this technique uses bandwidth more efficiently

Repeater: recover the digital data being transmitted, re-create an exact bit-for-bit copy of the original information, and retransmit the digital data, without the extraneous noise or electrical interference, at full strength towards the end destination

Router: a switching device in a packet-switched network that directs the transmission flow

Satellite: wireless broadband; Internet access via satellite signals; signals can only be beamed down to the user; cannot by transmitted back from the user

Server: a computer or software on a computer in a network accessible by the client machines of multiple users that returns files, print services, email, etc. in response to user requests

Switch: switches create interconnection in a network by directing the signals to their proper destinations

T-1, T-2, and T-3 lines: dedicated high-speed, high-capacity network links

TDM: time division multiplexing; assigns data streams to different timeslots

Transmission Media: any material substance or "free space," (i.e., a vacuum) that can be used for the propagation of energy in the form of pulses or variations in voltage, current, or light from one point to another; includes guided and unguided media

Twisted-pair Copper Wires: two wood-pulp or plastic-insulated copper wires twisted together in a pair

Unguided Transmission Media: gas, vapor, atmosphere; that in which boundary effects between free space and material substances are absent

WAN: wide area network; communications networks that cover a wide geographical area with indefinite distances

Contents

Sample Forms of Agreement

BLEC's Form Access Agreement

ACCESS AGREEMENT

THIS ACCESS AGREEMENT (the "Agreement") is made and entered into as of this ___ day of _____, _____ (the "Effective Date") by and between _____ (the "Licensor") and _____ (the "Licensee").

A. Licensee intends to install, operate, maintain, repair and replace hardware and systems necessary to provide the capability of providing high speed Internet access and other Internet-related communication services at the building located at _____ (the "Building").

B. Licensor desires to provide to Licensee use of certain portions of the Building to allow Licensee to provide such communication services, all on terms and conditions described below.

NOW, THEREFORE, in consideration of the mutual covenants contained herein and for good and valuable consideration, the receipt and sufficiency of which are hereby acknowledged, the parties hereto, intending to be legally bound, agree as follows:

BASIC PROVISIONS

Effective Date:		
Term:	**Renewal Term:**	**Terms of:**
Licensor:		
Licensor's Address for Notice:		
Licensee:		
Licensee's Address for Notice:		
Licensor's Representative:		

TERMS AND CONDITIONS

1. Grant of License. Licensor grants to Licensee a non-exclusive license to use certain interior space in the Building in accordance with the Plans as set forth in Section 9 below (the "Interior Space"). Further, Licensor grants to Licensee the right to use the pathways, shafts, risers, raceways, conduits, available telephone closets, interior communications wiring and cabling, service areas and utility connections and entries into and through the Building (collectively, the "Pathways"), for the purpose of providing communications services to the tenants and other occupants of the Building (collectively, the "Occupants"). Licensee may install Licensee's communications cabling, wiring and associated equipment, as more particularly described in Exhibit A attached to this Agreement (collectively, the "Equipment") in close proximity to the Building's inside wiring and cabling (i.e. the Building's "main distribution frame") for the purpose of connecting the Equipment to the main distribution frame. Licensee's right to install, operate, maintain, repair, relocate, upgrade and replace the Equipment shall be subject to the terms and conditions of this Agreement.

2. Term. Beginning on the Effective Date, this Agreement shall continue for the Term as set forth in the Basic Provisions chart above. Renewal Terms, as set forth in the Basic Provisions chart above, shall be automatically exercised without notice, unless Licensee provides notice of Licensee's intention not to renew at least three (3) months prior to the end of the then-current Term or Renewal Term. Each Renewal Term shall be on the same terms and conditions as such applying to the Term.

3. Compensation.
   3.1   Revenue Sharing.
         3.1.1 <u>Access Revenue</u>. Licensor shall be compensated at the rate of either _____ percent (___%) of the Access Revenue (as defined below) or _____ Dollars ($_____), whichever is greater. Access Revenue is defined as gross monthly recurring revenue received by Licensee from Occupants for the delivery of communications services, provided, however, such gross monthly recurring revenue shall exclude: (i) any one-time fee paid by any Occupant (by way of example, but not intending to limit the generality of the foregoing, any installation fees and/or any fees for any moves, adds or changes relating to the communication services provided to Occupants; (ii) any refundable deposits and any sums invoiced, collected and paid out for any sales, rental, use or excise tax or other governmental or regulatory tariffs, charges or fees or rebates payable by Licensee on account of the sale or delivery of communications services to the Occupants; and (iii) the amount of

any bad debt or uncollectible credit accounts with respect to the delivery of communication services to the Occupants previously taken into account in computing gross monthly recurring revenue.

3.1.2 <u>Licensor's Audit Rights</u>. Licensor shall have the right, at Licensor's expense and upon reasonable advance notice and during regular business hours, through a certified public accountant reasonably acceptable to Licensee, to examine the records maintained by Licensee regarding compensation of Licensor. Such right shall be exercisable no more than once every twelve (12) months. If the auditor discovers a discrepancy in amounts owed by Licensee to Licensor, Licensee shall pay to Licensor the amount of the discrepancy within thirty (30) days from the date upon which Licensee received from Licensor a written notice stating such discrepancy. If such discrepancy exceeds ten (10) percent of the total amount owed by Licensee to Licensor hereunder through the date of completion of the audit, Licensee also shall pay to Licensor the reasonable expense of the audit.

3.1.3 <u>Payment</u>. Licensee shall provide Licensor with annual reports of Access Revenue within thirty (30) days after the expiration of the relevant period. In the event that the total of the payments of Access Revenue for any calendar year is not equal to the annual amount of Access Revenue due and payable to Licensor under this Agreement, then Licensee shall pay to Licensor any deficiency by March 31 of the following year. Access Revenue payments shall be made by United States mail, postage prepaid to such address as may be specified by Licensor to Licensee in writing at any time in the future or to Licensor's address as specified in Section 15 below. Except as specifically set forth herein, all amounts payable hereunder shall be paid quarterly in arrears.

3.1.4 <u>Licensor's Books and Records</u>. To facilitate Licensor's right to audit, Licensee shall keep an accurate set of books and records of all Access Revenue derived from business conducted in the Building, and all supporting records such as tax reports, banking records, work orders and other sales records which are necessary to verify and substantiate Access Revenue at Licensee's headquarters. All such books and records shall be retained and preserved for at least thirty (30) months after the end of the calendar year to which they relate.

3.2 Stock Warrant.

3.2.1 <u>Grant</u>. Upon execution of this Agreement, Licensee shall issue to Licensor a stock purchase warrant in the form attached to this Agreement as <u>Exhibit B</u> (the "Warrant"). Licensor shall be entitled to exercise Licensor's rights under the Warrant in accordance with the terms and conditions thereof.

3.2.2 <u>Investment Representations</u>. Licensor understands that neither the Warrant nor the shares issuable upon exercise of the Warrant (the "Warrant Shares") have been registered under the Securities Act of 1933, as amended (the "Securities Act"). Licensor also understands that the Warrant is being offered and sold pursuant to an exemption from registration contained in the Securities Act based in part upon Licensor's representations contained in this Agreement. Licensor hereby represents and warrants as follows:

(i) <u>Acquisition for Own Account</u>. Licensor is acquiring the Warrant, and upon exercise of the Warrant, the Warrant Shares for Licensor 's and Licensor's affiliates' own account for investment only, and not with a view towards their distribution. By executing this Agreement, Licensor further represents that Licensor does not have any contract, undertaking, agreement or arrangement with any person to sell, transfer or grant participations to such person or to any third person, with respect to the Warrant or the Warrant Shares.

(ii) <u>Disclosure of Information</u>. Licensor and Licensor's advisors, if any, have been furnished with all materials relating to the business, finances and operations of the Company and materials relating to the offer and acquisition of the Warrants which have been requested by Licensor or Licensor's advisors. Licensor and Licensor's advisors, if any, have been afforded the opportunity to ask questions of the Company and receive responses to such questions. Licensor understands that Licensor's investment in the Warrants involves a significant degree of risk.

(iii) <u>Licensor Can Protect Licensor's Interest</u>. Licensor represents and acknowledges that by reason of Licensor's, or of Licensor's management's, business or financial experience Licensor is able to fend for itself, can bear the economic risk of Licensor's investment in securities of companies in the development stage, and has such knowledge and experience in financial or business matters that Licensor is capable of evaluating the merits and risks of the investment in the Warrant and the Warrant Shares. Licensor also represents Licensor has not been organized for the purpose of acquiring the Warrant.

(iv) <u>Accredited Investor</u>. Licensor is an "accredited investor" within the meaning of Securities and Exchange Commission ("SEC") Rule 501 of Regulation D, as presently in effect.

(v) <u>Restricted Securities</u>. Licensor understands that the Securities which Licensor is purchasing are characterized as "restricted securities" under the federal securities laws inasmuch as they are being acquired from the Company in a transaction not involving a public offering and that under such laws and applicable regulations such Securities may be resold without registration under the Act only in certain limited circumstances. In the absence of an effective registration statement covering the Securities or an available exemption from registration under the Act, the Securities must be held indefinitely. In this connection, such Licensor represents that Licensor is familiar with SEC Rule 144, as presently in effect, and understands the resale limitations imposed thereby and by the Act, including without limitation the Rule 144 condition that current information about the Company be available to the public. Such information is not now available, and the Company has no present plans to make such information available.

(vi) <u>Residence</u>. The office or offices of Licensor in which Licensor's investment decision was made is located at the address or addresses of Licensor set forth under Licensor's signature.

4. Electricity. Licensee shall pay to Licensor a monthly fee of _____ Dollars ($___) for the use of electricity in connection with Licensee's operations. Licensor shall have the right to audit Licensee's actual electrical usage. In the event that the actual usage exceeds _____ Dollars ($___) per month, Licensee shall remit to Licensor the difference between the actual amount of electricity consumed and _____ Dollars ($___), and in the event _____ Dollars ($___) per month constitutes an overpayment by Licensee, Licensor shall provide a credit or refund.

5. Personal Property Taxes. During the Term and any Renewal Term, Licensee shall be responsible for payment of all personal property taxes assessed directly upon and arising solely from Licensee's use of the Equipment in the Building. Licensee shall provide Licensor with timely evidence satisfactory to Licensor that all taxes due and payable for Licensee's personal property have been paid. Licensee shall have no responsibility for real estate taxes or assessments attributable to the Building.

6. Access. Beginning on the Effective Date, Licensee, Licensee's authorized employees, contractors, subcontractors or agents shall have access to the Building, without charge, during normal business hours upon at least twenty-four (24) hours prior verbal notice to Licensor, and at all other times in cases of emergency without notice to Licensor. In the case of an emergency, Licensee may enter or seek access to the Pathways through mechanical rooms or service areas, provided Licensee uses Licensee's reasonable efforts to give Licensor at least two (2) hours prior verbal notice and provided that, if practicable, a Building security guard or engineer shall unlock and accompany Licensee into such service areas and mechanical rooms. Notwithstanding the foregoing, Licensee shall reimburse Licensor for all costs incurred by Licensor as a result of after hours access to the extent such expenses are reasonable in accordance with commercial practices in the geographical area where the Building is located. Licensor shall assure Licensee access necessary for the operation and maintenance of the Equipment and associated utilities. In the event that the existing Pathways become unsuitable for Licensee's use or are fully utilized during the Term or any Renewal Term, Licensee may, at Licensee's expense, construct additional Pathways with Licensor's approval, which approval shall not be unreasonably withheld, conditioned or delayed.

7. Entry by Licensor. Licensee shall permit Licensor or Licensor's employees, agents or representatives to inspect any portion of the Interior Space and Pathways at all reasonable hours (and in emergencies at all times) to inspect the same, to clean or make repairs, alterations or additions thereto. However, Licensor shall not be obligated to change or delay Licensor's intended entry into these mechanical areas for this purpose and Licensee shall make a representative available to accompany Licensor on such inspection on the schedule desired by Licensor provided that Licensor has given Licensee notice of such entry at least two (2) days prior to such entry.

8. Use. Licensee shall use the Interior Space, Pathways and Equipment for the transmission and reception of communications signals (and for uses incidental thereto) and for the purpose of providing communications services to Occupants. Any use of the Interior Space, Equipment and Pathways by anyone other than Licensee (or Licensee's subcontractors or agents that perform installation or maintenance services for Licensee's Equipment) or Licensee's permitted assigns shall, unless otherwise agreed to by Licensor in writing, give Licensor the right to terminate this Agreement. Licensee shall not permit any other telecommunications provider or other third party to use—in whole or in part—Interior Space, Equipment and Pathways for any purpose (other than as necessary to enable Licensee to provide Licensee's communications services to Occupants), nor shall Licensee engage in co-location or provide co-location or interconnection services (it being understood and agreed that the foregoing provision is intended to prohibit Licensee from facilitating interconnections between third parties, other than as necessary to enable Licensee to provide Licensee's communications services to Occupants). Licensee shall not use or permit the use of the Interior Space, Equipment and Pathways for any purpose which is illegal, dangerous to life, limb or property or which creates a nuisance or which would increase the cost of insurance coverage with respect to the Building. In particular, no semiconductors or other electronic equipment containing polychlorinated biphenyl's (PCB's) or other environmentally hazardous materials shall either be used or stored in or around the Interior Space and Pathways and no such materials shall be used in any of the Equipment installed by Licensee in the Interior Space and Pathways. Licensee shall not permit unauthorized persons with insufficient expertise or experience to enter mechanical rooms in which the Interior Space, Equipment and Pathways are located and maintained or operate Licensee's Equipment. The mechanical rooms must be kept locked and secure at all times and the mechanical rooms must not be available or open to the public. Licensor may, at Licensor's discretion, authorize any Occupants or other parties, such as competing telecommunications service providers, to use portions of other vertical and/or horizontal spaces and pathways within the Building, whether for the installation of telecommunications equipment or otherwise, provided that, notwithstanding the foregoing, Licensor shall not permit any Occupants or other third parties that rely on the existing copper wires of the Building for transmission of internet communications and information services to the Building to use any space within the Building. Licensee shall obtain all licenses and permits required to install and operate the Equipment and otherwise comply with this Agreement, and Licensor shall cooperate with Licensee in connection therewith.

9. Installation. Prior to the installation of the Equipment and any alteration or upgrade thereto, Licensee shall deliver to Licensor the plans and specifications (the "Plans") therefor to obtain Licensor's reasonable approval. Licensor shall approve or reject the Plans, in writing, within fifteen (15) days after receipt thereof. If Licensor fails to approve or reject the Plans, in writing, within the fifteen (15) day period, then the Plans shall be deemed approved by Licensor. If Licensor rejects the Plans, Licensor shall state the reasons therefor in sufficient detail so that Licensee can modify the Plans and secure Licensor's approval. Licensee shall perform Licensee's work in a safe manner consistent with generally accepted construction standards. Licensee shall be responsible for such work and for the satisfaction or bonding of any lien filed by any provider of materials or services to Licensee. Licensee may connect into the Building's electrical utility system. Licensee shall keep the Building free from any liens arising out of any work performed, material furnished, or obligations incurred by Licensee relating to the Interior Space and the Pathways. If any claim of lien is recorded, Licensee shall bond against or discharge the same within thirty (30) days after Licensee's receipt of written notice that the same has been recorded against the Building.

10. Equipment. The Equipment and any other personal property of Licensee in the Building shall belong to Licensee and may be removed by Licensee at any time at Licensee's cost. Licensor shall not relocate any of the Equipment without Licensee's prior written approval, which approval shall not be unreasonably withheld, delayed or conditioned. Notwithstanding the foregoing, Licensee shall not be required to relocate any of the Equipment until the relocated equipment area is operational for Licensee's operations before disconnecting service from the original location.

11. Holding Over. If Equipment remains at the Building beyond thirty (30) days after the expiration or earlier termination of this Agreement without specific prior written approval from Licensor, Licensee shall, beyond such thirty-day period, pay to Licensor monthly license fees equal to the following percentages of the actual Access Revenue in effect and paid to Licensor immediately prior to the expiration or termination of this Agreement:

Month 1, 2 and 3	125%
Month 4, 5 and 6	150%
Thereafter	200%

12. Condition of Building. Licensee accepts the Interior Space and Pathways "as is" without benefit of any improvements to be constructed or made by Licensor. Licensor makes no representation or warranty regarding the Interior Space and Pathways. All installations or upgrades of the Equipment shall be performed in strict accordance with Licensor's reasonable requirements as communicated to Licensee from time to time.

13. Care and Maintenance by Licensee. Licensee shall maintain the Interior Space in a clean, attractive condition, commensurate with the other buildings in the geographic area in which the Building is located, unless such maintenance is necessitated by the acts or omissions of the Licensor or any Occupants or their respective employees, agents, subcontractors or contractors. At the end of the Term or any Renewal Term, Licensee shall remove the Equipment, shall repair any damage caused by such removal, and shall return the Interior Space in the same condition as received, normal wear and tear excepted.

14. Damages from Certain Causes. Neither party shall be liable to the other party for any loss or damage to any property or person occasioned by theft, fire, act of God, public enemy, injunction, riot, strike, insurrection, war, and, provided that such party is complying with its obligations hereunder, court order, requisition, or order of government body or authority.

15. Repairs and Alterations by Licensor. After receipt of notice by Licensee to repair or replace any damage to the Building, Interior Space or Pathways caused by Licensee or Licensee's agents or employees and failure of Licensee to commence such repairs within ten (10) business days following receipt of such notice, Licensor shall have the right, at Licensor's option and at Licensee's cost and expense, to repair or replace any damage done to the Building, or any part thereof, caused by Licensee or Licensee's agents or employees. Licensee shall not make or allow to be made any alterations to the Interior Space and Pathways without the prior written consent of Licensor, which consent shall not be unreasonably withheld or delayed.

16. Termination. Licensee shall have the right to terminate this Agreement upon thirty (30) days written notice for the following reasons: (a) Licensee determines that the Interior Space is not appropriate for Licensee's communications operations for economic or technological reasons; (b) through no fault of Licensee, Licensee encounters interference with Licensee's operations as a result of the use of any equipment operated at the Building by Licensor or any other party which equipment is installed subsequent to the installation of Equipment in the Building; (c) Licensor breaches any obligation hereunder and such breach is not remedied for thirty (30) days after delivery of written notice thereof from Licensee provided, however, that if such default cannot reasonably be cured within the thirty (30) day period, Licensor shall have additional time as may be necessary to cure such default so long as Licensor has commenced and is diligently pursuing the remedies necessary to cure such default; (d) hazardous or toxic materials (including, but not limited to, asbestos) not disclosed by Licensor in the Interior Space and the Pathways are found; or (e) through no fault of Licensee and despite commercially reasonable efforts by Licensee to the contrary, any license, permit or zoning variance required by Licensee (i) is not obtained (ii) expires (and may not be renewed) or (iii) is withdrawn.

17. Events of Default/Remedies. Any one or more of the following shall constitute an event of default by Licensee under this Agreement: (i) Licensee shall fail to pay any amounts due Licensor under this Agreement and such failure shall continue for a period of thirty (30) days after the date such sum is due and after written notice of such failure is received by Licensee; (ii) Licensee shall fail to comply with any material provisions of this Agreement or any other agreement between Licensor and Licensee not requiring the payment of money and such failure shall continue for a period of thirty (30) days after written notice of such default is received by Licensee, provided, however, if such condition cannot reasonably be cured within such thirty (30) day period, it instead shall be an event of default if Licensee shall fail to commence to cure such condition within such thirty (30) day period and/or shall thereafter fail to prosecute such action diligently and continuously to completion within a reasonable time period following receipt of Licensor's notice of default, (iii) the license hereunder granted shall be taken on execution or other process of law in any action against Licensee; (iv) Licensee shall become insolvent or unable to pay Licensee's debts as they become due, or Licensee notifies Licensor that Licensee anticipates either condition; (v) Licensee takes any action to, or notifies Licensor that Licensee intends to file a petition under any section or chapter of the United States Bankruptcy Code, as amended from time to time, or under any similar law or statute of the United States or any State thereof, or a petition shall be filed against Licensee under any such statute; or Licensee notifies Licensor that Licensee knows such a petition will be filed (but such events shall constitute an event of default under this License only to the extent permitted by law); or (vi) a receiver or trustee shall be appointed for Licensee's license interest in this Agreement or for all or a substantial part of the assets of Licensee. Upon the occurrence of any event or events of default by Licensee, Licensor shall have the option to pursue any remedies available to Licensor at law or in equity without any additional notices to Licensee or demand for possession whatsoever. Licensor's remedies shall include, but not be limited to, the right to terminate this Agreement in which event Licensee shall surrender the Interior Space and Pathways to Licensor.

18. Indemnification. Licensor and Licensee each agree to indemnify and hold harmless the other party from and against any and all claims, damages, costs and expenses, including, without limitation, reasonable attorney fees to the extent caused by or arising out of (a) the negligent acts or omissions or willful misconduct of the indemnifying party or the employees, agents, contractors, licensees, tenants and/or subtenants of the indemnifying party, or (b) a breach of any obligation of the indemnifying party under this Agreement, provided, however, this indemnification shall not extend to indirect, special, incidental or consequential damages, including, without limitation, loss of profits, income or business opportunities to the indemnifying party or anyone claiming through the indemnifying party.

19. Limitation on Recourse. Licensee's sole recourse against Licensor for the recovery of any judgments from Licensor shall be limited to the equity of Licensor in the Building and not to Licensor personally. The provisions contained in the preceding sentences are not intended to, and shall not, limit any right that Licensee might otherwise have to obtain injunctive relief against Licensor or relief in any suit or action in connection with enforcement or collection of amounts which may become owing or payable under or on account of insurance maintained by Licensor. Licensor's sole recourse against Licensee for the recovery of any judgments from Licensee shall be limited to the sum of the Access Revenue actually collected by Licensee during the twelve (12) month period preceding the date of the judgment and not to Licensee personally.

20. Insurance. Licensee shall obtain and maintain comprehensive general liability insurance coverage of no less than $1,000,000 per occurrence and $2,000,000 in the aggregate and commercial property insurance against all risk of direct physical loss or damage to the Equipment and Licensee's other personal property. Prior to commencing any work in the Building, Licensee shall provide to Licensor: (i) endorsements to the liability policies of Licensor and any subcontractors naming Licensor as additional insured; and (ii) certificates of insurance or copies of such insurance policies. Licensor and Licensee hereby waive any claims each might otherwise have against the other (or anyone claiming through or under them) on account of property damage (even if caused by negligence) if such damage is covered by any policy of insurance. Licensor and Licensee shall request their respective property insurance policies to include a waiver of the insurer's right of subrogation against the other. The insurance required by this Paragraph shall, without liability on the part of Licensor for premiums thereof, include the following: thirty (30) days prior notice of cancellation, non-renewal or material changes to the terms of coverage to each named insured; and waiver of subrogation rights. Further, the comprehensive general liability insurance shall also include an endorsement providing that the insurance afforded under Licensee's policy is primary insurance as respects Licensor and that any other insurance maintained by Licensor is excess and non-contributing with the insurance required of Licensee hereunder. Any type of insurance or any increase of its limits of liability not described above which Licensee requires for Licensee's own protection, or on account of statute, shall be Licensee's own responsibility and at Licensee's own expense. Should Licensee engage a contractor or subcontractor, the same conditions applicable to Licensee under this Agreement shall apply to each contractor or subcontractor, including, but in no way limited to, the indemnity and insurance clauses.

21. Assignment. Licensee may not assign or transfer this Agreement, or any interest herein, without the prior written consent of Licensor, which consent shall not be unreasonably withheld, conditioned or delayed. Notwithstanding the foregoing, Licensee may, without obtaining Licensor's consent, assign or transfer this Agreement to a parent or subsidiary or to any entity (a) which Licensee controls, is controlled by or is under common control with; (b) providing financing to Licensee; or (c) that succceeds to all or substantially all of Licensee's assets by purchase or merger; provided that (i) in any event Licensee shall not be released from liability pursuant to this Agreement; (ii) any assignee or transferee must execute an agreement whereby it assumes all obligations of Licensee under this Agreement and shall attorn to Licensor, and a copy of such agreement is provided to Licensor; and (iii) any such assignee or transferee must have a net worth that is equal to or greater than the net worth of Licensee as of the Effective Date.

22. Security. Licensor may elect to provide security services for Equipment to the Building during the Term or Renewal Term in a manner and to the extent which Licensor secures Licensor's own equipment in the Building and in such event, Licensee shall pay to Licensor a pro rata share of the cost of such security.

23. Building Rules. Licensee shall comply with the rules and regulations of the Building as reasonably adopted and altered by Licensor from time to time of which Licensee has received written notice and shall cause all of Licensee's agents, employees, invitees and visitors to do so. All changes to such rules shall be sent by Licensor to Licensee in writing.

24. Environmental. If any hazardous or toxic substances exist in the Building or are introduced to the Building by anyone other than Licensee during the Term or Renewal Term, Licensee shall have no obligation to remediate, abate or remove such hazardous or toxic substances, provided that Licensee is not responsible for the presence of such hazardous or toxic substances. Licensor shall indemnify and defend Licensee for any liability, cost or expense incurred by Licensee with respect to such hazardous or toxic substances that Licensee has not brought into the Building or disturbed in the Building. Licensee shall indemnify and defend Licensor for any liability, cost or expense incurred by Licensor with respect to such hazardous or toxic substances that Licensee has brought into the Building or disturbed in the Building. If Licensor becomes aware of the presence or precise location of any hazardous or toxic substances, including, but not limited to, asbestos, that are likely to affect Licensee's operations, Licensor shall promptly notify Licensee in writing of the presence and precise location thereof and Licensee may, in Licensee's sole discretion, immediately terminate this Agreement.

25. Compliance with Laws. Licensee shall comply with all applicable laws, ordinances, rules, and regulations of any governmental entity, agency or association having jurisdiction with respect to the Building, Licensee or Licensee's operations therein (collectively, the "Laws"). Licensor makes no representation that Licensee's contemplated use of Equipment, Interior Space and Pathways shall comply with applicable zoning or other laws, or with any public easements, covenants, conditions, restrictions, encumbrances or other matters of record (and this Agreement hereby is made expressly subject thereto).

26. Transfer by Licensor. Upon any sale, transfer or other disposition of the Building by Licensor, this Agreement shall be binding upon, and inure to the benefit of, the purchaser, transferee or grantee (collectively referred to as a "Purchaser") of the Building, and Licensor shall assign Licensor's interest under this Agreement to the Purchaser. Within ten (10) days after any sale, transfer or other disposition of the Building, Licensor shall notify Licensee of same and furnish to Licensee the name and address of the Purchaser thereof. A lease of all or substantially all of the Building shall be deemed a transfer within the meaning of this Section.

27. Casualty Damage. If the Interior Space or Pathways or any part thereof shall be damaged by fire or other casualty, Licensee shall give prompt written notice thereof to Licensor. In case the Building shall be damaged such that substantial alteration or reconstruction of the Building shall be required or in the event any mortgagee of Licensor's should require that the insurance proceeds payable as a result of a casualty be applied to the payment of the mortgage debt or in the event of any material uninsured loss to the Building or in the event Licensor determines that it is not economical or otherwise desirable to rebuild following a casualty which affects the provision of service under this Agreement, Licensor may, at Licensor's option, terminate this License by notifying Licensee in writing of such termination within thirty (30) days after the date of such casualty. If Licensor does not thus elect to terminate this License, Licensor shall commence and proceed with reasonable diligence to restore the Building shell and shell improvements located within the mechanical rooms in which the Interior Space or Pathways are located as well as restoration of the Pathways to the same condition in which they existed prior to damage by fire or other casualty; except that Licensor's obligation to restore shall not require Licensor to spend for such work an amount in excess of the insurance proceeds actually received by Licensor as a result of the casualty. Notwithstanding the foregoing, if the Building should become unsuitable for use by Licensee at any time during the Term or any Renewal Term of this Agreement due to fire or other casualty and Licensor does not restore such Building so as to permit resumption of operation by Licensee, this Agreement may be terminated by either party by giving written notice to the other party within ten (10) days following such casualty event. Access Revenue shall abate for so long as Licensee has ceased all or a portion of Licensee's operations providing communication services to Occupants as a result of any such casualty event.

28. Condemnation. If the whole or substantially the whole of the Building should be taken for any public or quasi-public use, by right or eminent domain or otherwise or should be sold in lieu of condemnation, then this Agreement shall terminate as of the date when physical possession of the Building are taken by the condemning authority. If less than the whole or substantially the whole of the Building are thus taken or sold, Licensor may terminate this Agreement by giving written notice thereof to Licensee; in which event this Agreement shall terminate as of the date when physical possession of such portion of the Building is taken by the condemning authority. If this Agreement is not so terminated upon any such taking or sale, Licensor shall, to the extent Licensor deems feasible, restore the Building to substantially their former condition, but such work shall not exceed the scope of the work done in originally constructing the Building and installing shell improvements in the Building, nor shall Licensor in any event be required to spend for such work an amount in excess of the amount received by Licensor as compensation for such taking. All amounts awarded upon a taking of any part or all of the Building shall belong to Licensor, and Licensee shall not be entitled to and expressly waives all claims to any such compensation. Notwithstanding the foregoing, if any Building should become unsuitable for use by Licensee at any time during the Term or any Renewal Term of this Agreement due to a taking or eminent domain proceeding so as to interrupt Licensee's operations, this Agreement may be terminated by either party by giving written notice to the other party within ten (10) days following such taking. Access Revenue shall abate for so long as Licensee has ceased all or a portion of Licensee's operations providing communication services to Occupants as a result of any such taking.

29. Notice to Tenants. Licensee shall notify Occupants of any interruptions to the communications services provided to such Occupants as follows:

(i) within twelve (12) hours following receipt by Licensee of notice of such interruption which causes any complete or material outage or failure of a service provided to an Occupant;

(ii) within twenty-four (24) hours following receipt by Licensee of notice of such interruption which limit the availability or functionality of a service provided to an Occupant in any non-material way.

30. Subscription Agreement Provisions. Licensee shall provide in each agreement with an Occupant subscribing for services from Licensee (each, a "Subscription Agreement") that the Licensor is not a service provider under such Subscription Agreement, is not related to Licensee in any way, shall be an intended thirty party beneficiary under the Agreement and shall have no responsibility or liability to the Occupant with respect to the provision, maintenance, failure or quality of any communications service received by such Occupant from Licensee pursuant to such Subscription Agreement. Licensee shall indemnify and hold harmless Licensor against any claims the Occupant may have against Licensor, provided that such claim arises out of and relates to only the services provided by the Licensee to the Occupant pursuant to the Subscription Agreement.

31. Lists of Tenants. Within thirty (30) days after the end of each calendar quarter, Licensee shall deliver to Licensor a list of all Occupants receiving communications services from Licensee and the duration of the applicable Subscription Agreement.

32. Cooperation. Licensee shall provide to Licensor and all Occupants receiving services from Licensee reasonable cooperation in the course of transition from Licensee to another service provider upon the expiration or earlier termination of this Agreement or the applicable Subscription Agreement. Further, Licensee shall exercise professional standard of care when dealing with Occupants.

33. Signage. Licensee shall not place signs on any of the doors or corridors leading to the Interior Space or Pathways, without first obtaining the prior written consent of Licensor in each such instance, which consent shall not be unreasonably withheld, conditioned or delayed. Licensor shall have the right, at Licensor's option, at Licensee's cost and expense, to remove any signs placed by Licensee without Licensor's prior written consent, and to repair any damage caused by such signs.

34. Severability. If any term or provision of this Agreement, or the application thereof to any person or circumstance shall, to any extent, be invalid or unenforceable, the remainder of this Agreement, or the application of such term or provision to persons or circumstances other than those as to which it is held invalid or unenforceable, shall not be affected thereby, and each term and provision of this Agreement shall be valid and enforced to the fullest extent permitted by law.

35. Time of the Essence. Except as otherwise stated herein, all times and dates are of the essence of this Agreement.

36. Subordination to Mortgage. Licensee accepts this Agreement subordinate to any mortgage, deed of trust or other lien presently existing or hereafter arising upon the Building, Interior Space or Pathway and to any renewals, modifications, consolidations, refinancing and extensions thereof, but Licensee agrees that any such mortgagee shall have the right at any time to subordinate such mortgage, deed of trust or other lien to this Agreement on such terms and subject to such conditions as such mortgagee may deem appropriate in its discretion. Licensor is hereby irrevocably vested with full power and authority to subordinate this Agreement to any mortgage, deed of trust or other lien now existing or hereafter placed upon the building and Licensee shall upon demand to execute such further reasonable instruments subordinating this Agreement or attorning to the holder of any such liens as Licensor may request. Licensee shall from time to time upon request by Licensor execute and deliver to such persons as Licensor shall request a statement in recordable form certifying that this Agreement is unmodified and in full force and effect (or there have been modifications, that the same is in full force and effect as so modified), stating the dates to which Access Revenue and other charges payable under this Agreement have been paid, stating that Licensor is not in default hereunder (or if Licensee alleges a default stating the nature of such alleged default) and further stating such other matters as Licensor shall reasonably require. Notwithstanding the foregoing, for the benefit of Licensee, Licensor shall use commercially reasonable efforts to obtain from Licensor's current or future mortgagee a Subordination, Non-Disturbance and Attornment Agreement (an "SNDA"), in which Licensee shall join, under which this Agreement and the rights of Licensee hereunder shall not be affected or modified by foreclosure or the exercise of any other right or remedy by the mortgagee so long as Licensee shall not be in default under any of the provisions of this Agreement beyond any applicable period of grace, and under which Licensee shall attorn to and recognize the mortgagee or any purchaser at foreclosure sale or other successor-in-interest to the Licensor as Licensee's licensor hereunder. Further, this Agreement shall be subject and subordinate to the lien of any mortgages hereafter placed upon the Building provided that the lender/mortgagee thereunder shall have executed an SNDA with Licensee whereby such lender agrees not to disturb Licensee in Licensee's rights, use and possession of the Building under this Agreement or to terminate this Agreement, notwithstanding the foreclosure or the enforcement of the mortgage or termination or other enforcement of an underlying lease or installment purchase agreement, except to the extent permitted by Licensor pursuant to the terms of this Agreement. The SNDA shall be in the reasonable form required by the lender and reasonably acceptable to Licensee. Licensee covenants and shall execute and deliver to Licensor or to the lender the SNDA within fifteen (15) business days after demand.

37. Recordation. Neither party to this Agreement shall record this Agreement. Either party may record a memorandum of this Agreement setting forth the basic information regarding this Agreement.

38. Amendment or Modification; Waiver. No provision of this Agreement may be amended or waived unless such amendment or waiver is agreed to in writing and signed by the Licensor and the Licensee. No waiver by any party hereto of any breach by another party hereto of any condition or provision of this Agreement to be performed by such other party shall be deemed a waiver of a similar or dissimilar condition or provision at the same time, any prior time or any subsequent time.

39. Entire Agreement. This Agreement embodies the entire agreement between the parties hereto with relation to the transaction contemplated hereby, and there have been and are no covenants, agreements, representations, warranties or restrictions between the parties hereto with regard thereto other than those specifically set forth herein.

40. Waiver and Approvals. Licensor hereby waives any and all lien rights, statutory or otherwise, in and to the Equipment. Licensor and Licensee hereby waive trial by jury in any action or proceeding brought by either against the other with respect to any matters connected with this Agreement. Any approval required hereunder shall not be unreasonably withheld, conditioned or delayed.

41. Notice. Unless otherwise specifically provided in this Agreement, any notice given under this Agreement shall be in writing and shall be delivered personally, sent by a nationally recognized air courier that provides confirmation of receipt by the recipient, such as Federal Express, or by United States certified mail, return receipt requested, postage prepaid. Each notice shall be addressed to the applicable party at the address as set forth in the Basic Provisions chart above. All notices to Licensee shall include a required copy to: Robert D. Lane, Jr., Esquire, Morgan, Lewis & Bockius LLP, 1701 Market Street, Philadelphia, PA 19103-2921. Notices shall be deemed received upon delivery or refusal thereof if personally delivered, on the first (1st) business day after delivery of such notice to a nationally recognized air courier if sent by such air courier or on the third (3rd) business day after deposit with the United States Postal Service if mailed as aforesaid. Either party may change its notice address by giving notice of such change in accordance with this Section.

42. Governing Law and Successors. This Agreement shall be governed by and construed under the laws of the state in which the Building is located, and shall be binding upon and inure to the benefit of the parties and their respective successors, transferees and assigns.

43.   Authority. Each party represents and warrants that it has the full power and authority to execute, deliver and perform under this Agreement. Licensor covenants that Licensee's use and enjoyment of the Equipment Space and Pathways shall not be disturbed by Licensor for the Term or any Renewal Term so long as Licensee is not in material default hereunder. Licensor represents that Licensor is either the owner of the Building or is duly authorized to execute this Agreement on behalf of such owner.

44.   Attorney's Fees. In the event that any action or proceeding brought by a party to this Agreement (a "Claimant") against the other party to this Agreement shall become final and non-appealable and decided in favor of the Claimant, then the other party to this Agreement shall pay the reasonable attorney's fees and expenses of the Claimant. In the event that any such action or proceeding brought by a Claimant shall become final and non-appealable against the Claimant, then the Claimant shall pay the reasonable attorney's fees and expenses of the other party.

45.   Contractors. All work to be performed on behalf of the Licensee hereunder shall be performed by reputable contractors or subcontractors.

46.   Requirements of Lenders. Licensee shall comply with the reasonable requirements of the lenders of Licensor; provided, that Licensee shall not be required to alter the terms of this Agreement or pay any additional fees to so comply.

47. Counterparts. This Agreement may be executed in counterparts, each of which shall be deemed to be an original but all of which together shall constitute one agreement.

LICENSOR: **LICENSEE:**

By: _____   By _____
        (Authorized Signature)   (Authorized Signature)
Name: _____   Name: _____

Title: _____   Title: _____

Date: _____   Date: _____

Address: _____

Building Owner's Form Access Agreement
ACCESS AGREEMENT

THIS ACCESS AGREEMENT (this "Agreement") is entered into this _____ day of _____, ____, between _____ a _____, having an office at _____ ("Licensor"), and _____, a _____corporation, having an office at _____ ("Licensee").

RECITALS:

WHEREAS, Licensee is in the business of (i) installing, managing and operating communications equipment within office buildings and office building complexes, and (ii) providing communications services, high speed Internet access and other Internet-related communication and services within, and for the benefit of multiple tenants and other occupants of, such buildings and complexes via such platforms, equipment and facilities;

WHEREAS, Licensor and Licensee desire to enter into this Agreement for the purpose of permitting Licensee to (i) install, operate, repair, relocate, upgrade, replace, manage and maintain such communications platforms, equipment and facilities within one or more buildings owned by Licensor and (ii) provide communications services to tenants and other occupants of such building(s) via such equipment;

WHEREAS, Licensor and Licensee each has the authority to enter into this Agreement and Licensor has the right, power and interest in the building(s) identified in this Agreement, which building(s) is (are) located on the land described in Exhibit A, hereto, to allow Licensee to make use of certain spaces within such building(s) as described in this Agreement.

NOW, THEREFORE, in consideration of the mutual covenants and obligations set forth herein, the parties hereto, intending to be legally bound hereby, agree as follows:

1. DEFINITIONS.

Unless otherwise defined herein, the following capitalized terms used herein shall have the respective meanings set forth below:

   (a)   "Approved Drawings" is defined in Section 6.1 below.
   (b)   "Approved Existing Wiring" is defined in Section 6.3 below.
   (c)   "Building" shall mean a building identified in the attached Exhibit B, located at the applicable address set forth therein.

(d)   "Buildings" shall mean all of the buildings identified in <u>Exhibit B</u>.

(e)   "Cable" shall be limited to unshielded or shielded twisted pair, copper wire, and related conduit and components necessary to deliver Communication Services from the Equipment Room to the Tenant Demarcation point.

(f)   "CLEC" shall mean a competitive local exchange carrier.

(g)   Commencement Date" shall mean the date upon which both parties have executed this Agreement.

(h)   "Communication Services" or "Services" shall mean high speed Internet access and other Internet-related communication services that Licensee may provide within a Building to Tenants of such Building subject to the terms of this Agreement, and may include all other services such as voice, video, data, facsimile or other communication services (or any combination of the foregoing) that Licensee may provide within a Building to Tenants of such Building subject to the terms of this Agreement. These Services may include, without limitation, (i) the provision and resale of local exchange services and point-to-point telephone communications (including dedicated long-distance service); (ii) video communications service; (iii) ?800? or other toll-free-number service; (iv) telephone credit or debit card service; (v) audio conferencing, paging, voice mail and message center service; (vi) data transmission service; (vii) access to computer "Internet" or other networked computer-based communications and related content, including access via Internet "portal" service; (viii) provision of telephone, video communication or other communications equipment or infrastructure to the users of such Services in connection with their use of such Services ("Tenant Equipment"); and (ix) any consulting or like telecommunications or Internet-related professional services.

(i)   "Controlled Items of Equipment" shall mean any item of Equipment that, during its normal operation, generates a significant amount of heat or consumes electric power in excess of one hundred ten volts (110v).

(j)   "Equipment" shall mean equipment used for the transmission of communications services, including (without limitation) Server(s), racks, cabinets, Cable, junction boxes, hangers, pull boxes, innerducts, connecting equipment, termination blocks, electrical wiring and related equipment, or any components thereof.

(k)   "Equipment Room" shall mean the space in the Building of not more than sixty (60) square feet in the location designated by Licensor and shown on the attached <u>Exhibit D</u>, which space shall be the location for items of Licensee's Equipment, as such Licensee's Equipment may be installed, replaced, supplemented, maintained, repaired, relocated, upgraded or substituted by Licensee from time to time in accordance with this Agreement. Licensor shall have no obligation to enclose, demise, or provide any security with respect to the Equipment Room or Licensee's Equipment.

(l)   "Existing Wiring" shall mean any Cable installed and maintained in a Building by an ILEC, CLEC, or other third party prior to January 1, 2000, and any other Cable owned by Licensor within such Building prior to January 1, 2000.

(m)   "GLA" shall mean, with respect to the Buildings that are the subject of this Agreement, the total square feet of rentable area within such Buildings, as determined prior to the date of this Agreement by Licensor. Licensor and Licensee hereby stipulate that, for all purposes of this Agreement, the total GLA of the Buildings is_____ square feet.

(n)   "Gross Sales," with respect to any Building, shall mean the gross amounts collected by Licensee on account of the provision or delivery of Services to Tenants within such Building, including any amounts collected in connection with granting the right to third parties to provide Services or content related thereto to Tenants (provided that using commercially reasonable accounting standards, such amounts are capable of being accounted for by Licensee), whether such gross amounts are collected from Tenants or otherwise (including payments for the sale, lease and upgrade of telephone equipment, but excluding installation charges and "moves, adds or changes," as such term is customarily used in the communications industry), whether Licensee delivers or performs the whole or any part of the Services from the Premises or from any other place within or outside the Building (but which Services are provided and received within the Building), and whether for cash, credit, in-kind, or other consideration. Gross Sales shall not, however, include any refundable deposits (unless and until Licensee takes such deposits into account as revenues other than as compensation or reimbursement for damage to Licensee's Equipment actually incurred) and any sums invoiced and collected and paid out for any sales, rental, use or excise tax or other governmental or regulatory tariffs, charges or fees or rebates payable by Licensee directly on account of the sale or rental of Services. Furthermore, there shall be deducted from Gross Sales (i) the amount of any bad debt or uncollectible credit accounts with respect to sales or rentals previously taken into account in computing Gross Sales (such deduction in any calendar year not to exceed one and one-half percent (1.5%) of the total Gross Sales for such calendar year), and (ii) credits for returned Tenant Equipment, the sale or rental of which previously had been taken into account in computing Gross Sales. Each sale upon installment or credit shall be treated as a sale for the full price in the quarter during which such sale is made irrespective of the time when Licensee receives payment therefor. Each credit against Gross Sales for uncollected or uncollectible credit accounts or for returned merchandise shall be applied in the quarter in which such account is written off by Licensee or such merchandise is returned; provided, however, that in the event any such account determined to be uncollectible should subsequently be collected by Licensee, any such amount so collected by Licensee shall be deemed a part of the Gross Sales for the quarter in which such amount is collected.

(o)   "Hazardous Materials" shall mean (i) any substance that now or in the future is regulated or governed by, requires investigation or remediation under, or is defined as a "hazardous substance," or otherwise as a toxic, explosive, radioactive, corrosive, flammable, carcinogenic, harmful, hazardous, or dangerous matter in the Comprehensive Environmental Response Compensation and Liability Act of 1980, 42 U.S.C. §§ 9601 et seq.; the Hazardous Materials Transportation Act of 1975, 49 U.S.C. §§ 31801 et seq.; the Resource Conservation and Recovery Act of 1975, 42 U.S.C. §§ 6901 et seq.; all as amended now or in the future; or any other federal, state, or local statute, law, ordinance, code, rule, regulation, order, or decree regulating, relating to, or imposing liability or standards of conduct concerning hazardous materials or waste or substances now or at any time hereafter in effect, or (ii) any liquid petroleum product, asbestos, PCB or formaldehyde.

(p)   "ILEC" shall mean an incumbent local exchange carrier.

(q)   "Initial Term" shall mean the period commencing on the Commencement Date and expiring on the date that is five (5) years after the Commencement Date.

(r)   ""Lateral/Station Cables" are those Cables located on a single floor of a Building that interconnect a Riser with a Service Provider Demarcation or a Tenant Demarcation within such Building.

(s)   "Laws" is defined in Section 8(e) below.

(t)   "License" is defined in Section 2.1 hereof.

(u)   "License Fees" shall mean the Percentage Fee and the Minimum Fee (as such terms are defined in Section 5.1 below), collectively.

(v)   "Licensed Areas" shall mean the Equipment Room, as such area may be modified from time to time pursuant to Approved Drawings.

(w)   "Licensee's Equipment" shall mean Equipment owned or leased by Licensee that may be installed in a Building in accordance with this Agreement, including, without limitation, such Equipment as Licensee may install in the Equipment Room, which shall not include Controlled Items of Equipment unless approved in writing by Licensor in advance of installation.

(x)   "Line Problems" shall mean and include any (i) eavesdropping, wiretapping, or theft of long distance or other access codes by unauthorized parties, (ii) failure of any of the Cable or Licensed Areas to satisfy Licensee's requirements, (iii) capacitance, attenuation, cross-talk, or other problems with Cable, (iv) misdesignation of the Cable or Existing Wiring in a Building, and (v) shortages, failures, variations, interruptions, disconnections, losses, or damages caused by or in connection with the installation, maintenance, replacement, removal, or use of any Equipment in the Building.

(y)   "Minimum Fee" is defined in Section 5.1 below.

(z)   "Non-Exclusive," with respect to the License granted by Licensor to Licensee pursuant to this Agreement, shall mean that Licensor may also authorize any other entities or persons to provide services similar to the Communication Services in the Building or Buildings.

(aa)   "Percentage Fee" is defined in Section 5.1 below.

(bb)   "Permitted Delays," with respect to the party claiming same, shall mean delays due to force majeure, as set forth in Section 27 of this Agreement.

(cc)   "Prevailing Market Percentage Rate" is as defined in Section 5.2 below.

(dd)   "Real Property" shall mean the land described in Exhibit A and the Buildings, the garage(s) of the Buildings, and the other improvements on such land (including any plazas and underground areas).

(ee)   "Renewal Term" shall mean the period commencing upon the expiration of the Initial Term of this Agreement and expiring on the day immediately preceding the tenth (10th) anniversary of the Commencement Date.

(ff)   "Risers" shall mean the vertical portions or segments of the Cable.

(gg)   "Rules and Regulations," with respect to any Building, shall mean the security, access, construction, operational, technical, sales, advertising, marketing, service and similar policies, standards, and guidelines (including requirements relating to contractor qualifications, procedures and insurance), as may be promulgated by the management of such Building, which Rules and Regulations may be modified from time to time in a nondiscriminatory manner. Notwithstanding the foregoing, Licensor shall not modify or amend the Rules and Regulations as a means of increasing the License Fees or materially increasing other charges payable by Licensee to Licensor under this Agreement.

(hh) "Server," with respect to any Building, shall mean a building-centric communications system installed, placed or maintained at any time in the Licensed Areas that has either (i) characteristics of private branch exchange service for voice and data transmission or (ii) characteristics of routing or switching equipment for Internet services, or (iii) both, and through which (or by means of which) two or more Tenants may obtain one or more Services.

(ii)   "Service Provider Demarcation" shall mean a location defined by any Laws, contract or custom where an ILEC or CLEC terminates its network within the Building.

(jj)   "Services" shall have the meaning set forth in Section 1(h) above.

(kk) "Subscription Agreement" shall mean a written agreement between Licensee and a Tenant pursuant to which such Tenant subscribes to receive any one or more Services from Licensee.

(ll)   "Telephone Closets" shall mean locations designated by Licensor within any Building at which interconnections between Lateral/ Station Cables, Tenant Demarcations, Risers, Service Provider Demarcations and related components are made. Telephone Closets may be located on each floor of a Building and may be designated by Licensor for common use by all communications service providers.

(mm) "Tenant Demarcation" shall mean the interface point between customer premises equipment of user Tenants, located within a Building, and Licensee's Equipment.

(nn) "Tenants" shall mean any tenants, subtenants, licensees or other occupants now or hereafter within a Building, but solely in their capacity as occupants of such Building.

(oo) "Term" shall mean, collectively, the Initial Term and, if extended pursuant to Section 4.2 of this Agreement, the Renewal Term.

(pp) "Undue Interference" shall mean an unreasonable or material, and adverse, disruption or interference.

(qq) "Work" shall have the meaning given such term in Section 6.1.

2. LICENSE.

2.1 Licensor hereby grants and conveys to Licensee the Non-exclusive right and license (but not an easement or any other interest in property), subject to the terms and conditions of this Agreement, to (a) construct, install, operate, maintain, manage, repair, reconstruct and replace Licensee's Equipment (including, without limitation, Licensee's Server), (b) use the Licensed Areas in the Buildings; and (c) market, sell and provide Licensee's Services within such Buildings, subject to Licensor's Rules and Regulations and the terms of this Agreement, solely for the purpose of providing Services to Tenants in the Buildings, and in any other building approved by Licensor in writing in advance, and for no other purpose whatsoever (the "License"). Subject to the terms and provisions of this Agreement, Licensee shall at all times during the Term have and enjoy the License and all other rights and interests hereby granted to Licensee under this Agreement (which shall not include any easement or other interest in property) without hindrance by Licensor or any person lawfully claiming through or under Licensor. It is expressly understood and agreed that Licensee shall not sublease or sublicense space within the Licensed Areas or Risers to other providers of telecommunications services for the purpose of permitting such providers to co-locate telecommunications equipment in such Licensed Areas or Risers.

2.2 The License granted by Licensor to Licensee under Section 2.1 above shall be Non-exclusive.

2.3 Licensee shall have the right to use and enjoy the Licensed Areas subject to and in accordance with this Agreement without charge from Licensor other than as expressly set forth in this Agreement.

2.4 Notwithstanding anything to the contrary contained herein, Licensor shall have the right to terminate this Agreement if Licensee has failed to install Licensee's Equipment in the Building on or before the date which is twelve (12) months after the Commencement Date.

3. ACCESS; NON-INTERFERENCE.

3.1 Subject to Licensor's Rules and Regulations applicable to a Building and provided that Licensee gives Licensor reasonable advance notice by telephone or otherwise, Licensee shall have the non-exclusive right, at Licensee's sole cost and expense, to enter upon the Licensed Areas, and such areas within the Building as necessary to reach the Licensed Areas, twenty-four (24) hours a day, seven (7) days a week, three hundred sixty-five (365) days a year, to conduct the activities described in Section 2.1 of this Agreement, including the installation, maintenance, repair, inspection, relocation and replacement of the Licensee's Equipment, and provided that Licensor shall have the right to be present to observe the activities of Licensee's authorized representatives, subject to Section 24 of this Agreement. Notwithstanding the foregoing, Licensor may condition any granting of access to Tenant space, whether emergency or otherwise, on compliance with the leases that are then in effect between Licensor and any such Tenants, and subject to any reasonable restrictions of such Tenants for security and privacy purposes.

3.2 If Licensor gives to Licensee prior written approval (which Licensor may not unreasonably withhold, condition or delay), and subject to any reasonable conditions or limitations imposed by Licensor, Licensee shall have the non-exclusive right to use Existing Wiring installed within a Building by parties other than Licensee to the extent that Licensor has the right to grant such access and right of use, provided that Licensee shall be solely responsible for obtaining any such right of access and right of use from any party from whom such rights are required other than Licensor. Licensor may require Licensee, by giving Licensee notice within fifteen (15) days after the Commencement Date, to use existing Risers within a Building, and not to install new Risers, to the extent such existing Risers (and the reasonable conditions and limitations imposed by Licensor with respect thereto) are reasonably suitable to Licensee's needs in performance and delivery of the Services to Tenants.

3.3 In connection with the installation and subsequent operation by Licensee of any of Licensee's Equipment, or Licensee's related use or occupancy of the Licensed Areas, Licensee shall not cause any impairment or Undue Interference with respect to the operation or use of communications facilities or equipment that were installed in the Buildings prior to the date of Licensee's installation causing such impairment or Undue Interference. In the event of any such impairment or Undue Interference caused by Licensee in violation of this Section 3.3, Licensee shall immediately remedy such condition, and if Licensee fails to do so within seventy-two (72) hours after receiving notice of such condition from Licensor or the affected occupant, Licensor shall be entitled to remedy such condition at Licensee's expense, and Licensee shall pay to Licensor the actual costs reasonably incurred by Licensor in providing a remedy for such impairment or Undue Interference within ten (10) days after receipt of Licensor's invoice therefor. Notwithstanding the foregoing, in the event that any such impairment or Undue Interference caused by Licensee results in an emergency situation, Licensor shall be entitled to remedy such condition immediately at Licensee's expense.

4. TERM.

4.1 The Term of this Agreement shall commence on the date of this Agreement and shall continue in effect so long as any Initial Term or Renewal Term remains in effect.

4.2 At the conclusion of the Initial Term, provided that Licensee is not then in default under this Agreement beyond applicable grace or cure periods expressly provided by this Agreement, the Term shall automatically be extended (without the necessity of any notice of election to cause such extension) for a Renewal Term of five (5) years, commencing on the expiration of the Initial Term, upon the same terms and conditions as set forth herein, except that the License Fee shall be adjusted as set forth in Section 5.2 below. Notwithstanding the foregoing, Licensee may, at its option, elect to terminate this Agreement as of the scheduled expiration date of the Initial Term by giving notice (the "Non-Renewal Notice") to Licensor of such election not less than three (3) months prior to the expiration of the Initial Term. If Licensee delivers the Non-Renewal Notice to Licensor at least three (2) months prior to such expiration, this Agreement shall automatically terminate as of the scheduled expiration date of the Initial Term.

5. LICENSE FEE.

5.1 In consideration of the granting to Licensee of its rights under this Agreement, Licensee shall pay a license fee with respect to each Building in the amount of the sum of five percent (5%) of Gross Sales for such Building for each calendar quarter during the Term (the "Percentage Fee"); provided, however, that in any event, commencing as of the first day of the fourth (4th) full calendar month of the Term, the license fee payable hereunder by Licensee shall not be less than the applicable amount set forth on Schedule 1 annexed hereto and made a part hereof per calendar month for such month and for each succeeding calendar month during the Term of this Agreement (the "Minimum Fee"), which Minimum Fee Licensee shall pay to Licensor, in advance, on the first (1st) day of each calendar quarter, without notice, demand, or invoice from Licensor. Licensee shall receive a credit against the Percentage Fee due for a calendar quarter for the amount of Minimum Fee paid by Licensee for such calendar quarter, as provided in Section 5.2 of this Agreement below.

5.2 With respect to each Building, commencing as of the first day of the Renewal Term, if any, the percentage rate used for purposes of determining the Percentage Fee payable by Licensee shall be the greater of (i) the then "Prevailing Market Percentage Rate" (as hereinafter defined) and (ii) five percent (5%) of Gross Sales. "Prevailing Market Percentage Rate" shall mean the then prevailing market percentage rate of revenue (based on definitions of "revenue" comparable to the definition of "Gross Sales" used in this Agreement) payable for a new license (or a renewal of an existing license) to provide services comparable to the License granted hereunder for a term that is comparable to the Renewal Term in office space comparable to the Building. The Prevailing Market Percentage Rate shall be determined between Licensor and Licensee by mutual agreement on or before the date that is two (2) months prior to the expiration of the Initial Term; however, if Licensor and Licensee cannot agree, the Prevailing Market Percentage Rate shall be established in the manner specified below in this Section 5.2. If Licensor and Licensee have not reached an agreement as to the Prevailing Market Percentage Rate on or before the date that is two (2) months prior to the expiration of Initial Term, Licensor and Licensee shall, within thirty (30) days after such date, each submit to the other its final determination of a proposed Prevailing Market Percentage Rate. If Licensor and Licensee shall be unable to agree on the Prevailing Market Percentage Rate, Licensor and Licensee shall jointly identify an expert who has significant experience in assessing the value of providing, on a commercial basis, services similar to the Services in multi-tenant office buildings (an "appraiser"), who shall make a final determination of the Prevailing Market Percentage Rate. In the event that Licensor and Licensee cannot agree on the appointment of an appraiser within thirty (30) days after submission of the both proposed figures, the Parties shall submit the matter to the American Arbitration Association ("AAA") for appointment of an appraiser. Within twenty (20) days after the appointment of such expert by the Parties or by the AAA, such expert shall select one of the determinations of the Prevailing Market Percentage Rate as submitted by Licensor and Licensee, as aforesaid, without modification or qualification. Any assessment by an expert of the Prevailing Market Percentage Rate shall consider the factors described above in the second (2nd) sentence of this Section 5.2. Licensor and Licensee agree that they shall be bound by the determination of Prevailing Market Percentage Rate pursuant to this Section 5.2 for the Renewal Term (which shall not be subject to further adjustment during such Renewal Term). Licensor and Licensee shall bear equally the fees and expenses of the appraiser, if any.

5.3 Within sixty (60) days after the end of each calendar quarter during the Term of this Agreement, Licensee shall pay to Licensor the amount by which the Percentage Fee for the immediately preceding quarter exceeds the total Minimum Fees previously paid to Licensor for that quarter. Within sixty (60) days after the expiration or earlier termination of this Agreement, Licensee shall pay to Licensor the amount by which the Percentage Fee for the portion of the quarter in which such expiration or termination occurs falling prior to such expiration or termination exceeds the total Minimum Fees previously paid to Licensor for that period. Within sixty (60) days after the end of each calendar quarter during the Term, Licensee shall submit to Licensor, with respect to each Building, an itemized, accurate written statement, certified by a duly authorized officer of Licensee, setting forth the full amount of Gross Sales for the subject Building during such quarter.

5.4 The acceptance by Licensor of payments of the Percentage Fee or Minimum Fee shall be without prejudice, and shall in no event constitute a waiver of Licensor's right to assert the existence of a deficiency in the payment of any such fee or to audit Licensee's books and records relating to Gross Sales. Licensee agrees to keep, retain and preserve at its address for notice hereunder for at least thirty-six (36) months after the expiration of each calendar year during the Term of this Agreement, complete and accurate books and records in accordance with generally acceptable accounting principles to determine or verify Gross Sales for each Building. Licensor may, from time to time during the Term of this Agreement, make an audit of the books and records of Licensee pertaining to the Gross Sales applicable to any or all Buildings. If any such audit shows a deficiency in the amount of Gross Sales reported by Licensee that is more than three percent (3%) of the amount of Gross Sales reported by Licensee for the period of the audit, and as a result thereof, any License Fee is due and owing, then (in addition to payment of any delinquent Percentage Fee) Licensee shall pay to Licensor, within thirty (30) days after written demand from Licensor, the actual, reasonable costs and expenses of such audit up to an amount equal to such License Fee deficiency. Except as aforesaid, any audit shall be conducted solely at Licensor's cost and expense.

5.5 Notwithstanding the provisions of this Section 5 to the contrary, the License Fees paid by Licensee to Licensor shall be in addition to, and not in lieu of, the stock warrants issued to Licensor in accordance with the Warrant Agreement.

6. CONSTRUCTION AND INSTALLATION.

6.1 Prior to commencing any construction, installation or material modification of Equipment and related improvements within a Building (collectively, "Work"), Licensee shall submit detailed specifications, plans and drawings related to such Work to Licensor, for Licensor's information and prior written approval. Licensor shall respond to such request for approval within the period requested by Licensee in such submittal, which period shall not in any event be less than fifteen (15) business days after Licensor's receipt thereof, and Licensor shall not unreasonably withhold or condition any such requested approval; provided, however, that with respect to (a) Work on or affecting roof-top space, (b) Work that affects the Building's aesthetic appearance, structural integrity or mechanical, plumbing, electrical, heating, ventilation, air conditioning, life safety or other Building systems (including the addition of Equipment that would affect areas outside the Equipment Room due to heat loads), (c) Work that Licensee knows, or reasonably should know, involves the Building's asbestos procedures (provided that Licensee has received a copy of such procedures), and (d) Work that involves the installation, replacement or substantial modification of any generator, fuel tank or battery, Licensor may withhold, condition, or delay its approval in its sole discretion. In addition, Licensor shall promptly advise Licensee in writing if any Work proposed by Licensee will require Licensor to incur any costs or expenses that may be payable by Licensee in accordance with Section 6.5 of this Agreement. If Licensee reasonably determines that any such costs or expenses, or any conditions or requirements imposed by Licensor in connection with such approval process, preclude or materially diminish the commercial viability of Licensee's operations in the Building, then Licensee may terminate this Agreement upon thirty (30) days' written notice to Licensor. The plans, specifications and drawings shall conform to Licensor's Rules and Regulations, applicable building codes and other Laws and shall be in sufficient detail as to enable Licensee's contractor to obtain all necessary governmental permits for commencement of the Work and to secure complete bids from qualified subcontractors to perform the Work. The approved plans and specifications or drawings shall be referred to herein as "Approved Drawings." Subject to Section 3.1 of this Agreement, Licensee shall have reasonable access to such Building(s) at such times and on such terms as Licensor may reasonably declare to conduct such Work. Licensor shall be entitled to make and retain copies of all such specifications, plans, and drawings submitted to Licensor. If the actual installation of any Licensee's Equipment does not comply in any material way with the Approved Plans, Licensee shall provide two (2) sets of "as built" drawings to Licensor in accordance with the Rules and Regulations promptly after completion of the applicable Work. Upon Licensor's request, Licensee shall also make available to Licensor Licensee's wire management information with respect to the Buildings.

6.2   All Work shall be (a) performed by Licensee (or a contractor approved by Licensor in writing) in accordance with Licensor's Rules and Regulations applicable to the Buildings, (b) performed in a workman-like manner, lien-free and in accordance with all applicable Laws, (c) without affecting or implicating the Building's asbestos procedures, and (d) in a safe manner consistent with sound construction standards and practices. No Work shall commence before delivery to Licensor of a certificate of insurance with respect to Licensee and the applicable contractor evidencing current insurance coverage in accordance with the requirements set forth in Section 12 of this Agreement (with respect to Licensee) or Licensor's Rules and Regulations (with respect to the contractor). All construction and installation of the Licensee's Equipment shall be at Licensee's sole cost and expense. In addition, upon the request of Licensor, Licensee shall provide such parties with copies of any required governmental and quasi-governmental permits, licenses, approvals and authorizations related to such Work and update such permits as required upon any expiration thereof.

6.3 Licensee shall, at the time of installation, clearly identify all Licensee's Equipment with labels, as required by the Building management. With respect to any Existing Wiring that Licensee uses with Licensor's approval pursuant to Section 3.2 above ("Approved Existing Wiring"), Licensee shall affix such identifying labels upon commencing its use of such Approved Existing Wiring. Licensee shall mark each line of Approved Existing Wiring used by Licensee with such identifying information and the starting point and destination of such Approved Existing Wiring (e.g. "No. _____, B1 to Floor 39"), and shall place such identification tags in each closet through which Approved Existing Wiring passes, and on each horizontal run of such Approved Existing Wiring.

6.4 Subject to this Agreement, Licensee's Equipment may be installed, replaced, supplemented, relocated, maintained, upgraded or substituted from time to time. From time to time during the Term, but in no event less frequently than semi-annually, Licensee shall provide Licensor with a current update of Licensee's Equipment installed in the Equipment Room.

6.5 If, and only to the extent that, Licensee's Work (but not Licensee's operations, which are subject to Section 8(e) below) requires Licensor to construct improvements in the Building in order to comply with applicable Laws, then, within ten (10) days after Licensee's receipt of an invoice from Licensor, Licensee shall reimburse Licensor all actual costs reasonably incurred by Licensor to repair such damage or comply with such Laws. Licensor shall give Licensee written notice of Licensor's estimate of the amount of such compliance costs. Licensor shall provide such notice prior to incurring such costs and shall state in the notice the anticipated commencement date of the compliance work, provided it is reasonably possible to compile such estimate and give such notice to Licensee in advance without substantial risk to Licensor of being cited or penalized for noncompliance with the applicable Laws. Licensor will use reasonable care in preparing the estimate, but it shall be a good faith estimate only and will not limit Licensee's obligation to pay for the actual compliance costs if Licensee proceeds with the relevant Work. If Licensee reasonably determines that the costs or expenses associated with any such Work, or any conditions or requirements imposed by Licensor in connection with such approval process, preclude or materially diminish the commercial viability of Licensee's operations in the Building, then Licensee may terminate this Agreement with respect to the affected Building upon thirty (30) days' written notice to Licensor.

6.6   Licensor reserves the right, at Licensor's sole discretion and expense, but not more than once during any consecutive twelve (12) month period, to require Licensee to relocate the Licensed Area, Licensee's Equipment or any space on the roof to a mutually agreeable area within the Building; provided, that any such area shall be sufficient to allow Licensee to provide the type, level and quality of services provided by Licensee prior to such relocation. Licensor agrees to allow Licensee reasonable time, not to exceed sixty (60) days, for such relocation. In this event, Licensor would make the "Substitute Licensed Area" and the Licensed Area available to Licensee concurrently to provide continuity to Licensee's telecommunications services. Upon presentation of appropriate supporting documentation, Licensor shall reimburse Licensee for its reasonable, actual out-of-pocket expenses incurred in connection with any such relocation.

7. UTILITIES.

7.1   Licensor shall make available to Licensee reasonable access to existing electrical power facilities in the Buildings to permit Licensee to provide electrical current connections necessary for Licensee's provision of Services to Tenants in the Buildings. Licensee shall pay to Licensor a flat fee at the rate of _____ Dollars ($___) per month per Building for the consumption of electricity within each of the Buildings. Licensor, at Licensor's option, may cause a reputable and independent electrical engineer or electrical consulting firm, selected by Landlord, to make a determination of the value of the electricity consumed by Licensee at each of the Buildings, by multiplying the demand and consumption of electric energy used by Licensee by the then-current electric rate charged to Licensor for the Building. If the value of the electricity consumed by Licensee as so determined shall exceed Fifty Dollars ($50.00) per month with respect to any Building, Licensee shall thereafter pay such increased amount with respect to such Building.

7.2   Except as specifically provided in this Section 7, Licensor shall have no obligation to provide any utilities or services to or for Licensee, the Licensed Areas, or the Equipment. For any additional services or utilities Licensee may require for performance and delivery of the Services in the Building(s), including (without limitation) heating, air conditioning, humidity control, ventilation, gas, water, fire sprinklers, alarm and security services, pest and rodent control, cleaning and trash removal, Licensee shall install any required equipment in the Licensed Areas and shall (a) if feasible, obtain such utilities and services directly from and pay for the same directly to, the applicable utility company, municipality, or service provider, and (b) obtain such other services from such contractors as Licensor uses generally at the Building, or such other contractors as Licensor shall approve in writing in advance, and in accordance with Licensor's Rules and Regulations applicable to the Building, and shall pay for the services provided by such contractors directly to such contractors.

    7.3 Licensor shall not be liable or responsible to Licensee for any loss, damage or expense which Licensee may sustain or incur as a result of any failure, fluctuation, outage, or interruption of electrical power or if the quantity, character, or supply of electrical energy is changed or is no longer available or fails at any time to be suitable for Licensee's requirements, except to the extent that any such change or failure is caused by the gross negligence or willful misconduct of Licensor.

8. LICENSEE'S COVENANTS.

With respect to each Building, Licensee hereby covenants and agrees as follows:

    (a) Licensee shall respond to any problems, complaints, or difficulties asserted by any Tenant with respect to any of the Services provided to such Tenant as follows:

        (i) within one (1) hour if in response to a major problem, complaint or difficulty, where "major" problems, complaints, and difficulties include, for example, problems that cause any complete or material outage or failure of a Service provided to a Tenant;

        (ii) within three (3) hours if in response to a minor problem, complaint or difficulty, where "minor" problems, complaints, and difficulties include, for example, problems that limit the availability or functionality of a Service provided to a Tenant in any non-material way; and

        (iii) within twenty-four (24) hours if in response to a purchase order signed by such Tenant for any "moves, adds or changes" (as such terms are customarily used in the communications industry).

    (b) Licensee shall install and keep the Licensee's Equipment in good order, repair and condition in accordance with maintenance standards promulgated by the manufacturer of the Equipment, if any, and shall promptly and adequately repair all damage to the Building or any property of any occupant or Licensor caused by Licensee or its authorized representatives, and restore such property to its condition prior to such damage, ordinary wear and tear, condemnation, damage, or destruction and Hazardous Materials not placed in the Buildings by Licensee (or in connection with the provision of the Services) excepted.

(c)   To the extent such numbering plan shall be applicable to Licensee and/or the Services, Licensee shall maintain compliance with the North American Numbering Plan (NANP) in connection with Licensee's provision of Services to Tenants.

(d)   Licensee, at its sole expense, shall comply with all Laws applicable to the Services or the Licensee's Equipment and the installation thereof (including, without limitation, all Laws pertaining to Licensee's installation, maintenance, operation, modification, replacement, removal or use of Licensee's Equipment and Licensee's use, repair or alteration of the Licensed Areas) and shall obtain and maintain all necessary and required permits, licenses, and authorizations relating thereto. For purposes hereof, the term "Laws" shall mean all federal, state, county, regional, municipal, utility commission, and other governmental laws, ordinances, orders, rules, and regulations, now or hereafter in effect. Licensor makes no representation that Licensee's contemplated use of Licensee's Equipment, Approved Existing Wiring, the Licensed Areas or any other portion of the Building will comply with applicable zoning or other Laws, or with any private or public easements, covenants, conditions, restrictions, encumbrances or other matters of record or not of record (and this Agreement is hereby made expressly subject thereto), and Licensee's violation of any of the same shall be a breach of this section 8(e). Licensee shall be solely responsible for obtaining, at Licensee's sole cost and expense, any necessary zoning or other governmental or private approvals, variances, special use permits or otherwise satisfying any such requirements (provided that in doing so Licensee shall not adversely affect Licensor or impair in any way Licensor's current and permitted use of the Building), and Licensor shall cooperate with Licensee in connection therewith at no cost to Licensor; provided, however, that Licensor makes no representation whatsoever that any of the foregoing items may be obtained, and any delays in Licensee's obtaining the same shall not delay the Commencement Date or Licensee's obligations under this Agreement. If, after commercially reasonable efforts, Licensee is unable to obtain any permit required for the operation of Licensee's business in any Building, or any applicable Laws or any of the other matters described above in this section 8(e) preclude or substantially impair such operations, then Licensee shall have the right to terminate this Agreement with respect to the affected Building upon thirty (30) days' advance notice to Licensor. If any physical operations of Licensee are conducted in a manner which has the effect of imposing any requirement on Licensor to comply or cause any portion of any Building or Real Property to comply with any Laws, Licensee shall be responsible for and shall pay to Licensor upon demand all costs of such compliance reasonably incurred by Licensor and caused by Licensee's manner of use, but only to the extent that Licensor would not otherwise be required to comply with any such Laws absent Licensee's operations in the Building (herein "Compliance Costs"). Licensor shall give Licensee written notice of Licensor's estimate of the amount of such Compliance Costs prior to incurring such costs and shall state in such notice the anticipated commencement date of the compliance work, provided it is reasonably possible to compile such estimate and give such notice to Licensee in advance without substantial risk to Licensor of being cited or penalized for noncompliance with the applicable Laws. Licensor will use reasonable care in preparing the estimate, but it shall be a good faith estimate only and will not limit Licensee's obligation to pay for the actual Compliance Costs reasonably incurred.

(e)　Licensee shall not disrupt, adversely affect or interfere with Licensor's operations or maintenance of the Building or any Tenant's use and enjoyment of its leased premises or of the common areas of the Building or Property.

(f)　Licensee shall not use or permit to be used any part of any Building for any dangerous, noxious, or offensive trade or business or for the generation, treatment, storage, or disposal of Hazardous Materials or release any of the foregoing in any Building;

(g)　Licensee shall provide in each Subscription Agreement (a form of which is annexed hereto as Exhibit D) that (i) the Licensor is not a service provider under such agreement, is not related to Licensee in any way, shall be an intended third party beneficiary under the agreement, and shall have no responsibility or liability to the Tenant with respect to the provision, maintenance, failure, or quality of any Service received by such Tenant from Licensee pursuant to such Subscription Agreement; (ii) any cessation or interruption of the Services shall not constitute a default or constructive eviction by Licensor under the leases between the Tenant and Licensor; and (iii) Tenant shall hold Licensor harmless from, and shall waive as against Licensor, any claims the Tenant may have against Licensee pursuant to such Subscription Agreement;

(i) Licensee shall deliver to Licensor, on a semi-annual basis, a list of all Tenants receiving Services from Licensee and the duration of the applicable Subscription Agreements, which information shall be subject to the confidentiality covenants and requirements of Section 19 below;

(j) Licensee shall install a 24-hour "critical eye" system connected to Licensee's Server in the Building that automatically detects any deviation from the standard operation thereof and notifies a network operations center of such deviation;

(k) Licensee shall use commercially reasonable efforts to install a redundant or diverse system, including appropriate safety and security measures to safeguard Licensee's Equipment, to provide robust operations and a minimum level of Services to Tenants in the event Licensee's primary system fails;

(l) Licensee shall install in the Building(s) only "Year 2000 compliant" Servers and other Licensee's Equipment that may contain microprocessors or any other date-sensitive logic, which shall mean, for purposes of this Agreement, that the hardware, software, or system forming any part of such Licensee's Equipment shall receive, process, and produce date-related data without error resulting from any data or input containing dates before, on, or after January 1, 2000; and

(m) Licensee shall provide to Licensor and all Tenants receiving Services from Licensee reasonable cooperation in the course of transition from Licensee to another Services provider upon the expiration or termination of this Agreement or the applicable Subscription Agreement, including participation in a reasonable cutover procedure designed to maintain continuous service to such Tenants.

9. CASUALTY DAMAGE; EMINENT DOMAIN.

If any Building should become unsuitable for use by Licensee at any time during the Term of this Agreement due to fire or other casualty, or a taking by eminent domain, Licensor shall not be required to restore such Building so as to permit resumption of operation by Licensee. In the event of any such unsuitability, this Agreement may be terminated by either party by giving written notice to the other party within ten (10) days following such casualty event or taking and not less than thirty (30) days prior to the termination date specified in such notice. License Fees shall abate for so long as Licensee has ceased all operations providing Services to Tenants as a result of any such casualty event or taking. Notwithstanding anything herein to the contrary, no termination of this Agreement under this Section 9 or for any other reason shall cause a termination of any other license agreement between Licensor and Licensee.

10. RISK OF LOSS; REMOVAL OF EQUIPMENT; NO SUITABILITY WARRANTIES.

10.1 The presence of the Equipment and any other personal property of Licensee within any Licensed Areas or other portion of a Building shall be at the sole risk of Licensee, and Licensor and its members, partners, officers, directors, employees, and affiliates shall not be liable for damage thereto or theft, misappropriation or loss thereof, except to the extent caused by the gross negligence or willful misconduct of Licensor or its affiliates, or their agents or employees. Within ninety (90) days after the expiration or earlier termination of this Agreement, Licensee shall, unless otherwise agreed by Licensor and Licensee, remove all of Licensee's Equipment from the Building at Licensee's sole cost and expense. Licensee shall repair any damage caused by installation and such removal of Licensee's Equipment, ordinary wear and tear, condemnation, damage, or destruction and Hazardous Materials not placed in the Buildings by Licensee (or in connection with the provision of the Services) excepted. Any such Licensee's Equipment not so removed within ninety (90) days after the expiration or earlier termination of this Agreement may, at Licensor's option and upon written notice to Licensee, (i) be removed and disposed of by Licensor within ninety (90) days thereafter, at Licensee's reasonable cost and expense, or (ii) be deemed the property of Licensor, at no further cost, expense or liability to Licensee.

10.2 If Licensee fails to remove Licensee's Equipment within the ninety (90) day period described in Section 10.1 above, Licensee shall pay to Licensor as liquidated damages, and not as a penalty (it being agreed by the Licensor that the actual damages suffered by Licensor would be difficult to ascertain and that the following liquidated damages represent a reasonable estimate under the circumstances), on a monthly basis, an amount determined in accordance with the following table, or the highest amount permitted by Law, whichever shall be less, for any period in which Licensee shall retain possession of the Licensed Areas or any part thereof or any other portions of the Building after expiration or earlier termination of this Agreement (and any failure by Licensee to disconnect from and discontinue using, or if required by Licensor any failure to remove, any Communications Equipment following written demand for the same by Licensor pursuant to the provisions of this Agreement shall constitute continuing possession for purposes hereof).

Period of Holdover (number of days after the ninety (90)-day period described in section 10.1 above)	Liquidated Damages (as a percentage of the greater of (i) the then-current License Fee or (ii) the then-current fair market rental for the affected space)
1 through 29	150%
30 through 59	200%
60 through 89	250%
90 or more	300%

The provisions of this Section 10.2 shall not serve as permission for Licensee to hold over, nor serve to extend the term of this Agreement (although Licensee shall remain bound to comply with all provisions of this Agreement until Licensee surrenders the Licensed Areas). Licensee's obligations under this Section 10.2 shall survive the expiration or earlier termination of this Agreement.

10.3 Licensor makes no warranty or representation that any Building is suitable for the use contemplated by this Agreement, it being assumed that Licensee has satisfied or will satisfy itself as to the suitability of such space. Prior to executing this Agreement, Licensee has inspected the Building(s) and accept the same "as is," and Licensee hereby agrees that Licensor are under no obligation to perform any work or provide any materials to prepare the Building(s) for Licensee, except as provided in this Agreement.

11. PUBLIC ANNOUNCEMENTS.

11.1 Except as permitted in writing by Licensor in its sole discretion, Licensee shall not, and shall not permit its employees, agents, contractors or other persons authorized by Licensee to, publish or distribute any advertisement, brochure, press release, public announcement or other similar communication that: (a) makes any reference to Licensor or any of its affiliates, or the Building, except for the street address and, to the extent Licensor is legally entitled to permit the same, the trademark or other legal name, of the Buildings, (b) states that Licensor or any of its affiliates endorses or recommends Licensee's products or services, (c) states that Licensee has any exclusive right to provide such products or services at the Buildings, (d) uses any picture or likeness of the Buildings or any other properties owned or managed by Licensor or its affiliates, or (e) is materially inaccurate or misleading, or adversely affects the reputation of the Buildings or Licensor or its affiliates.

12. INSURANCE; INDEMNITY.

12.1 Licensee shall defend, indemnify, and save Licensor, its affiliates, trustees, beneficiaries, general and limited partners, and members, and the officers, directors, and employees thereof (collectively with Licensor, the "Indemnified Parties") harmless from and against any and all (a) liens, claims, liabilities, damages, losses, costs, and expenses, including reasonable expert's and attorney's fees, arising from or by reason of the installation, placement, maintenance, repair, operation, use, and/or removal of Licensee's Equipment in, on, or from the Real Property (physical damage to the Real Property resulting from ordinary wear and tear, condemnation, damage, or destruction and Hazardous Materials not placed in the Buildings by Licensee (or in connection with the provision of the Services) excepted), (b) breaches or defaults by Licensee in the performance of any covenant or agreement on the part of Licensee to be performed pursuant to the terms of this Agreement, (c) acts of Licensee, its agents, contractors, or employees in or about each Building, (d) all damages, losses, judgments, settlements, costs, and expenses, including reasonable expert's and attorney's fees, arising out of any claims by and against any person related to Line Problems, provided such Line Problems are not related to Risers that Licensee is obligated to use pursuant to Section 3.2 of this Agreement, and (e) Licensee's provision or alleged failure to provide Services to any Tenant. Notwithstanding the foregoing, Licensee shall not have any obligation under this Section 12.1 respecting any liens, claims, liabilities, damages, losses, costs and, expenses to the extent caused by the gross negligence or willful misconduct of Licensor or its agents, employees or contractors (other than Licensee).

12.2 Licensee shall, at Licensee's expense, maintain during the term of this Agreement (and, if Licensee shall occupy or conduct activities in or about any portion of the Building prior to or after the Term hereof, then also during such pre-Term or post-Term period): (a) commercial general liability insurance including contractual liability coverage, with a minimum coverage of One Million Dollars ($1,000,000) per occurrence/Two Million Dollars ($2,000,000) general aggregate per location, plus a Five Million Dollars ($5,000,000) umbrella per location, for injuries to, or illness or death of, persons and damage to property occurring in or about the License Areas or otherwise resulting from Licensee's operations in the Building, (b) property insurance protecting Licensee against loss or damage by fire and such other risks as are insurable under then-available standard forms of "special coverage" insurance policies (excluding earthquake and flood but including water damage), covering Licensee's Equipment and any other Licensee property in or about the Licensed Areas or the Real Property and also covering any fixtures that may belong to Licensee and any improvements or alterations, for the full replacement value thereof without deduction for depreciation; (c) workers' compensation insurance in statutory limits; and (d) at least three months' coverage for loss of business income and continuing expenses, providing protection against any peril included within the classification "special," excluding earthquake and flood but including water damage. All such policies shall provide coverage on an "occurrence" rather than a "claims made" basis. The above-described liability policies shall protect Licensee, as named insured, and Licensor and all the Indemnified Parties and any other parties designated by Licensor, as additional insureds; shall insure Licensor's and such other parties' contingent liability with regard to acts or omissions of Licensee; shall specifically include blanket contractual liability coverage (provided, however, that such contractual liability coverage shall not limit or be deemed to satisfy Licensee's indemnity obligations under this Agreement); and shall be primary to, and not contributing with, any liability policies carried by such additional insureds. Licensor reserves the right to increase the foregoing amount of liability coverage from time to time as Licensor determines, in the exercise of its reasonable discretion, taking into account applicable industry norms, is required to protect adequately Licensor and the other parties designated by Licensor from the matters insured thereby. Any such modification of Licensor's insurance requirements, procedures or protocol must be exercised and applied by Licensor with respect to all similarly situated occupants and licenses in the Building in a nondiscriminatory manner. Nothing in this Section 12 shall be construed as creating or implying the existence of (i) any ownership by Licensee of any fixtures, additions, alterations, or improvements in or to any portion of the Building or (ii) any right on Licensee's part to make any addition, alteration, or improvement in or to any portion of the Building.

12.3 Each insurance policy required pursuant to this Section 12 shall be issued by an insurance company licensed to do business in the state in which the Building is located and with a general policyholders' rating of "A" or better and a financial size ranking of "Class VIII" or higher in the most recent edition of Best's Insurance Guide, or any equivalent rating service if Best's Insurance Guide is discontinued or revised. Each insurance policy, other than Licensee's workers' compensation insurance, shall (a) provide that it may not be materially changed, cancelled, or allowed to lapse unless thirty (30) days' prior written notice to Licensor and any other insureds designated by Licensor is first given, and (b) provide that no act or omission of Licensee shall affect or limit the obligations of the insurer with respect to any other insured. Such insurance may be carried under a policy or policies covering other liabilities and locations of Licensee; provided, however, that the insurance coverage and the amounts available to the location of the Real Property shall not ever be less than the amounts specified in Section 12.2. From time to time, Licensee shall furnish Licensor such evidence as Licensor may require to indicate that the foregoing insurance is in full force and effect and the premiums have been paid. Each such insurance policy or a certificate thereof shall be delivered to Licensor by Licensee on or before the effective date of such policy and thereafter Licensee shall deliver to Licensor renewal policies or certificates at least thirty (30) days prior to the expiration dates of expiring policies. If Licensee fails to procure such insurance or to deliver such policies or certificates, Licensor may, at its option, procure the same for Licensee's account, and the cost thereof shall be paid to Licensor by Licensee upon demand.

12.4 By executing this Agreement, each party hereto hereby releases the other party and, in the case of Licensee as the releasing party, the other

Indemnified Parties identified in Section 12.1 above, and the respective partners, shareholders, agents, employees, officers, directors and authorized representatives of such released party, from any claims such releasing party may have for damage to the Building, the Licensed Areas or any of such releasing party's fixtures, personal property, improvements, and alterations in or about the Licensed Areas, the Building, or the Real Property, or for loss of revenue due to business interruption that is caused by or results from risks insured against under any property and business interruption insurance policies actually carried by such releasing party or deemed to be carried by such releasing party; provided, however, that such waiver shall be limited to the extent of the net insurance proceeds payable by the relevant insurance company with respect to such loss or damage, plus the amount of any deductible or self-insured retention thereunder. For purposes of this Section 12.4, Licensee shall be deemed to be carrying any of the insurance policies required pursuant to this Section 12 but not actually carried by Licensee, and Licensor shall be deemed to carry the property insurance and rental loss coverage required by the holders of any Superior Interest, or if there is no Superior Interest encumbering the Buildings, then a standard special coverage property and business interruption policy with respect to the Real Property and Licensor's business operations therein consistent with the coverage normally carried by commercially reasonable landlords of comparable commercial buildings in the city in which the Building(s) is/are located. Each party hereto shall cause each such property insurance policy and business interruption insurance policy obtained by it to provide that the insurance company waives all rights of recovery by way of subrogation against the other respective party and the other aforesaid released parties in connection with any matter covered by such policy. Each such party shall indemnify the other party from and against any loss or expense, including reasonable attorneys' fees, resulting from the failure to obtain the waiver required under this Section 12.4. The provisions of this Section 12.4 are paramount and shall control any conflict with any other provisions of this Agreement.

13. LIENS.

Licensee shall not permit the creation of any security interest in or other encumbrance upon any Building or any other property of Licensor, or the attachment or encumbrance of any mechanic's, materialman's or other lien against any Building or any other property of Licensor, as a result of any Work or provision of Services by or on behalf of Licensee. Licensee shall indemnify and hold Licensor and its Affiliates harmless from and against any such liens, including reasonable attorneys' fees and costs. Any such lien shall be removed or bonded over by Licensee within thirty (30) days after Licensee's receipt of notice of attachment thereof, unless otherwise agreed to by Licensor. If any such lien is not removed or bonded over by Licensee within such period, Licensor may take such reasonable and necessary action to remove the same, and the reasonable cost thereof, including reasonable attorneys' fees and expenses actually incurred, shall be immediately due and payable from Licensee to Licensor.

14. EVENTS OF DEFAULT.

The occurrence of any one or more of the following shall constitute an "Event of Default" under this Agreement:

(a) The breach by either party of any material provision of this Agreement, and failure to cure such breach within thirty (30) days after receipt of written notice thereof from the non-breaching party, provided that for any breach that is curable but cannot reasonably be cured within such thirty (30) day period, in which case the breaching party must begin to cure such Event of Default within such thirty (30) day period and diligently pursue such cure until completion (and provided, further that with respect to matters which do not pose a health, safety or security risk and do not annoy Tenants of the Building, the period within which the breaching party must cure or commence to cure the breach, as described above, shall be thirty (30) days);

(b) Licensee commences a voluntary proceeding under the Federal Bankruptcy Code, or any action or petition is otherwise brought by Licensee seeking similar relief or alleging that it is insolvent or unable to pay its debts as they mature; or any action is brought against Licensee seeking its dissolution or liquidation of any substantial portion of its assets, or seeking the appointment of a trustee, interim trustee, receiver, or other custodian for any substantial portion of its property, and any such action is consented to or acquiesced in by Licensee or is not dismissed within three (3) months after the date upon which it is instituted.

(c) Licensee's failure to pay any portion of the Percentage Fee, the Minimum Fee, or other charges payable to Licensor (including any interest accrued under this subparagraph) on or before the date on which the same becomes due and payable, and such payment is not made for a period of ten (10) days following receipt by Licensee of written notice from Licensor. Licensee shall also pay to Licensor a late charge equal to one and one-half percent (1.5%) per month on all amounts not timely paid, which late charge shall accrue from the date due until the delinquent sums are paid in full; provided, however, with respect to amounts paid as a result of any audit by Licensor of Gross Sales as provided in Section 5.4, such late charge shall not commence accruing until the fifth (5ᵗʰ) business day after Licensee's receipt of Licensor's invoice therefor and shall not accrue with respect to any portion of the invoiced amounts which Licensee ultimately and successfully challenges. Further, notwithstanding the foregoing, (i) if Licensor has given Licensee notice of a monetary default twice within any 12-month period, then the late charge on such delinquent amount shall be three percent (3.0%) per month, and (ii) in no event shall the total liability for the late charge exceed the applicable limits, if any, imposed by Laws. Any late charge in excess of such limits shall be refunded to Licensee or credited toward any sums then due from Licensee.

(d) The notice and cure periods herein are in lieu of, and not in addition to, any notice and cure periods provided by Laws.

15. REMEDIES.

15.1 Upon the occurrence of an Event of Default by Licensee, Licensor shall have, in addition to any rights or remedies expressly provided herein or otherwise available at law or in equity, the right to (a) terminate this Agreement upon thirty (30) days' notice to Licensee, in which event Licensee shall immediately surrender the Licensed Areas to Licensor and remove Licensee's Equipment in accordance with Section 10.1 or (b) enter upon the Licensed Areas and do whatever Licensee is obligated to do under the terms of this Agreement, and Licensee agrees to reimburse Licensor on demand for any costs and expenses reasonably incurred by Licensor in effecting compliance with Licensee's obligations under this Agreement.

15.2 Upon the occurrence of an Event of Default by Licensor, Licensee shall have, in addition to any rights or remedies expressly provided herein, the right to (i) terminate this Agreement upon thirty (30) days' written notice to Licensor, and thereafter to remove the Licensee's Equipment in accordance with Section 10.1, (ii) seek equitable relief (exclusive of self-help remedies), or (iii) in the event of any default due to Licensor's gross negligence or willful misconduct, sue for actual damages. Notwithstanding the foregoing, Licensee hereby covenants that, prior to the exercise of any such remedies, Licensee will give the holder of any Superior Interest of which Licensor has given Licensee notice pursuant to this Agreement (which notice, in order to be effective for this purpose, must include the address of such holder to be used for notices) notice and a reasonable time to cure any default by Licensor, commensurate with the associated cure period afforded Licensor under this Agreement.

16.   ASSIGNMENT; SUBORDINATION.

16.1 Except as expressly permitted under Section 16.2 below, Licensee may not, by operation of Law or otherwise, transfer, assign, sublicense or encumber all or any portion of its rights and obligations under this Agreement to another person or entity (collectively, an "assignment") without the prior written consent of Licensor, which consent may not be unreasonably withheld, conditioned or delayed. Any attempted assignment, sublicense or transfer without consent as required above (except as permitted in Section 16.2) shall be void and shall be deemed an Event of Default by Licensee.

16.2 Notwithstanding the foregoing, however, Licensee may assign this Agreement, or its rights hereunder, to (a) any corporation, company or other entity controlling, controlled by, or under common control with Licensee, (b) any partnership in which Licensee has a controlling interest, or (c) any person or entity which succeeds to substantially all of Licensee's assets (provided such purchaser shall have also assumed substantially all of Licensee's liabilities) provided (i) Licensee notifies Licensor at least thirty (30) days prior to such assignment, (ii) such assignee executed an agreement whereby it assumes all obligations of Licensee under this License and agrees to attorn to Licensor, (iii) a copy of such agreement is promptly provided to Licensor, and (iv) such assignee shall have the financial and operational ability to perform the obligations under this License, as determined by Licensor in its reasonable discretion. For the purposes hereof, control shall mean the direct or indirect ownership of fifty percent (50%) or more of the voting rights of, and beneficial interest in, the entity in question and the power to direct or cause the direction of the management and policy of the entity in question.

16.3 Licensee shall pay to Licensor, as Licensor's cost of processing each proposed assignment or sublicensing, an amount equal to the sum of Licensor's actual out of pocket expenses reasonably incurred in connection with such proposed assignment or sublicensing, including without limitation reasonable attorneys' and other professional fees.

16.4 Without limiting any of the provisions of this Section 16 of the Agreement, if Licensee has entered into any sublicenses of any portion of the Licensed Areas, the voluntary or other surrender of this Agreement by Licensee, or a mutual cancellation by Licensor and Licensee, shall not work a merger, and shall, at the option of Licensor, terminate all or any existing sublicenses or, at the option of Licensor, operate as an assignment to Licensor of any or all such sublicenses. If Licensor does elect that such surrender or cancellation operate as an assignment of such sublicenses, Licensor shall in no way be liable for any previous act or omission by Licensee under the sublicenses or for the return of any deposit(s) under the sublicenses that have not been actually delivered to Licensor, nor shall Licensor be bound by any sublicense modification(s) executed without Licensor's consent or for any advance rental payment by the sublicensee in excess of one month's rent.

16.5   This Agreement and any renewal hereof are expressly made subject and subordinate to any mortgage, deed of trust, ground lease, underlying lease or like encumbrance affecting any part of the Real Property or any interest of Licensor therein which is now existing or hereafter executed or recorded, any present or future modification, amendment or supplement to any of the foregoing, and to any advances made thereunder (any of the foregoing being a "Superior Interest") without the necessity of any further documentation evidencing such subordination. Notwithstanding the foregoing, Licensee shall, upon Licensor's request, execute and deliver to Licensor a document evidencing the subordination of this Agreement to a particular Superior Interest. If the interest of Licensor in the Real Property or the Building is transferred to any person ("Purchaser") pursuant to or in lieu of proceedings for enforcement of any encumbrance, Licensee shall, at the Purchaser's election, attorn to the Purchaser and this Agreement shall continue in full force and effect as a direct agreement between the Purchaser and Licensee on the terms and conditions set forth herein.

17.   NOTICES.

Every notice required or permitted hereunder shall be in writing and shall be deemed to have been duly given when delivered by hand, mailed by certified or registered mail, return receipt requested, or sent by recognized overnight or same-day delivery service, to the party's address set forth below. Notices shall be deemed given upon receipt, except that any correctly addressed notice that is refused, unclaimed or undeliverable because of an act or omission of the party to be notified shall be considered to be effective as of the first date that the notice was refused, unclaimed or considered undeliverable by the postal authorities, messenger or courier service. Either party may change its address for the purpose of notice hereunder by providing to the other party notice of such change of address. In addition to the foregoing, Licensor may contact Licensee at the following telephone number twenty-four (24) hours per day, seven (7) days a week respecting emergencies relating to the performance of Services hereunder (which number Licensee may change from time to time by giving notice to Licensor as provided above): (For convenience of communication only, and not for purposes of satisfying the notice requirements under this Agreement, set forth below are fax numbers of each of the parties.)

If to Licensor:

_____
_____
_____
Attention:_____
Fax No.:_____

If to Licensee:

_____
_____
_____
Attention:_____
Fax No.:_____

18.   RULES AND REGULATIONS.

Licensee shall comply with all Rules and Regulations promulgated by Licensor with respect to any Building; provided, however, that with respect to any conflict between such Rules and Regulations and the express provisions of this Agreement, this Agreement shall control.

19.   CONFIDENTIALITY.

The terms and conditions of this Agreement constitute confidential information of Licensor and Licensee. All information provided by Licensor to Licensee relating to its customers, tenants, business strategies, marketing plans, technology, finances, and personnel, and all other information shall constitute confidential information. Except as may be required to be disclosed by Law or court order or pursuant to the rules or requirements of any securities commission or exchange, and subject to the exclusions set forth below, all confidential information received under this Agreement shall be maintained in confidence by the recipient, through the exercise of the same level of care the recipient uses with respect to its own confidential information of similar sensitivity (but in no event less than a reasonable degree of care) to avoid any unauthorized disclosure to, or access by, any third party other than the accountants, attorneys, employees, agents, and representatives of the recipient and its affiliates who have a need to know the information for purposes of this Agreement and who have obligations of confidentiality with respect to the confidential information received hereunder commensurate with the obligations set forth in this Section 19. Notwithstanding the foregoing, Licensor and Licensee may disclose the existence and general nature of the relationship between the parties to this Agreement and either party may use any or all of the provisions of this Agreement in any other license agreement that either of them might enter into with third parties, so long as specific references to any Building, Licensor, or Licensee is not made in such other agreement.

20. GOVERNING LAW.

This Agreement shall be governed by and construed in accordance with the internal laws of the state in which the Building that is the subject of any dispute or question of law is located.

21. HAZARDOUS MATERIALS.

21.1 If Licensor becomes aware of the presence and precise location of any Hazardous Materials, including asbestos, that are likely to significantly and adversely affect Licensee's Services or Licensee's Equipment, Licensor shall promptly notify Licensee in writing of the presence and precise location thereof. If Licensee encounters any materials that Licensee determines to be Hazardous Materials, Licensee shall promptly notify Licensor of such event, and Licensee shall not proceed with any Work in the area containing such materials without prior written authorization from Licensor with respect to such Work. With respect to Hazardous Materials that Licensor has identified for Licensee, in accordance with this Section 21.1, or of which Licensee knows or reasonably should know, Licensee shall handle any such materials in accordance with applicable environmental and safety laws and Licensee shall indemnify Licensor against all claims, liabilities and losses arising from Licensee's failure to do so. If any Hazardous Materials are found in the Buildings, Licensor shall not be required by this Agreement to remove, abate, or remediate the Hazardous Materials; provided, however, that (a) if Licensor elects to do so, Licensor shall be solely responsible for any such removal, abatement, and remediation of the same it chooses to undertake, including any environmental assessments and any clean-up of the Buildings or Licensee's Equipment located therein which may be contaminated, and Licensee shall not be responsible for any such removal, abatement or remediation or the costs or expenses associated therewith, and (b) if, and only to the extent that, any such elective removal, abatement or remediation substantially interferes with Licensee's operations in the Building, including Licensee's provision of Services to Tenants, the License Fee payable by Licensee hereunder shall equitably abate during the period of such interference.

21.2 Licensee will not store, use, generate, release, or dispose of any Hazardous Materials in, on, or about any Building nor will Licensee cause or permit its agents, employees, or contractors to do so. No semiconductors or other electronic equipment containing Hazardous Materials will either be used or stored by Licensee in or around any Building and no such materials will be used in any of the Equipment installed by Licensee in any Building, except as expressly permitted under environmental laws, regulations and guidelines governing same. Notwithstanding the forgoing, Licensee may use batteries, which may contain environmentally sensitive materials, as a back-up power supply for certain items of its Equipment. Such batteries will be installed, maintained, and removed by Licensee in accordance with all applicable Laws and Section 6 above, and will be the sole responsibility of Licensee. If Licensee breaches this Section 21.2, or if Licensee, its agents, employees, or contractors introduce any materials to any Premises or Building which result in the contamination of such Premises or Building, and such materials are Hazardous Materials at the time of installation or introduction thereof, then Licensee shall indemnify, defend and hold Licensor and Licensor's Affiliates harmless from any and all claims, judgments, damages, penalties, fines, costs, liabilities, or losses (including reasonable expert's and attorneys' fees actually incurred) which arise as a result thereof. Notwithstanding anything herein to the contrary, however, Licensee shall not have any responsibility for managing, monitoring or abating, nor be the owner of, nor have any liability for, any Hazardous Materials that Licensee, its agents, contractors or employees have not brought into a Building or disturbed in such Building in contravention of Licensee's covenants and obligations under this Section 21 and Section 6 above.

22.   ENTIRE AGREEMENT; MODIFICATIONS.

This Agreement, which includes all exhibits and attachments incorporated by reference or attachment, contains the entire agreement of the parties with respect to its subject matter and supersedes any prior or contemporaneous agreements or understandings with respect to such subject matter. The terms and conditions of this Agreement may not be modified, amended, or waived, except by an instrument in writing signed by both parties.

23.   SEVERABILITY.

If any clause or provision of this Agreement is or becomes illegal, invalid or unenforceable because of present or future laws or any rule or regulation of any governmental body or entity, effective during the Term, the intention of the parties hereto is that the remaining parts of this Agreement shall not be affected thereby.

24.   ACCESS BY LICENSOR.

Licensee shall not interfere with Licensor, or its employees, agents, or representatives, in their access to any portion of the Building and Licensed

Areas at all times to inspect the same or to clean or make repairs, alterations, or additions thereto, and Licensee shall not be entitled to any abatement or reduction of License Fees by reason thereof.

25. LIMITATION OF LIABILITY.

25.1   Licensee shall neither assert nor seek to enforce any claim for breach of this Agreement, or otherwise, against any of Licensor's assets or against the assets of Licensor's managing agent, other than the interests of such parties in the Real Property, and the rents, issues, profits, and proceeds thereof, and Licensee agrees to look solely to such interest for the satisfaction of any liability of Licensor, or its managing agent under this Agreement or otherwise, it being specifically agreed that in no event shall Licensor, its Affiliate or managing agent (which terms shall include, without limitation, any of the officers, trustees, directors, partners, beneficiaries, joint ventures, members, stockholders, or other principals or representatives thereof, disclosed or undisclosed) ever be personally liable for any such liability.

25.2   Licensor shall neither assert nor seek to enforce any claim for breach of this Agreement, or otherwise, against any of the assets of any of the officers, trustees, directors, partners, beneficiaries, joint ventures, members, stockholders, or other principals or representatives of Licensee, disclosed or undisclosed, it being agreed that no such persons or entities shall ever be personally liable for any such liability.

25.3   In no event shall either party to this Agreement, or such party's agents or employees (or any of the officers, trustees, directors, partners, beneficiaries, joint ventures, members, stockholders, or other principals or representatives thereof and the like, disclosed or undisclosed) ever be liable for indirect, special, consequential, punitive, or incidental damages of the other party arising out of this Agreement.

26. NO IMPLIED WAIVER.

The failure of either party to insist at any time upon the strict performance of any covenant or agreement herein or to exercise any option, right, power or remedy contained herein shall not be construed as a waiver or a relinquishment thereof. No provisions of this Agreement shall be waived by Licensor or Licensee unless such waiver is in a writing signed by the party giving such waiver. The waiver by either party of any breach of any provision of this Agreement by the other party shall not be deemed a waiver of any subsequent breach of the same or any other provision of this Agreement. No payment by Licensee of a lesser amount than the monthly installment of Percentage Fees or Minimum Fees due hereunder shall be deemed to be other than on account of the earliest of such fees due hereunder, nor shall any endorsement or statement on any check or any letter accompanying any check or payment be deemed an accord and satisfaction, and Licensor may accept such check or payment without prejudice to its right to recover the balance of such fees or pursue any other remedy or herein.

27. FORCE MAJEURE.

Licensee and Licensor shall be excused for the period of any delay in performance of any obligations hereunder by reason of labor disputes, civil disturbance, war, war-like operations, invasions, rebellion, hostilities, military or usurped power, sabotage, governmental regulations or controls, fires or other casualty, inclement or adverse weather of unusual amount or duration for the subject season, or acts of God. In order to be entitled to an excuse for any delay or failure to perform under this Agreement pursuant to this Section 27, the party claiming such excuse shall promptly give written notice to the other party hereto of any event or occurrence which the notifying party asserts to be within the contemplation of this Section 27 and shall exercise all reasonable efforts to remove the cause of such delay. This Section 27 shall not apply to the payment of the Percentage Fee, Minimum Fee, or any other monies due hereunder. In no event will insufficient funds constitute an event of force majeure.

28. COMMISSIONS.

Each party to this Agreement indemnifies and holds the other harmless against any loss, claim, expense, or liability (including, without limitation, court costs and attorneys' fees) with respect to any commissions or brokerage fees claimed on account of the execution and/or renewal of this Agreement, or expansion of equipment space hereunder, if applicable, due to any action of the indemnifying party. Licensor acknowledges that Licensor is not owed any commissions or brokerage fees from Licensee in relation to the negotiation or execution of this Agreement.

29. MODIFICATIONS.

Any modification of this Agreement or any additional obligations assumed by either party in connection with this Agreement shall be binding only if evidenced in writing, signed by each party.

30. RECORDATION.

This Agreement is not in recordable form and the parties hereto shall not record or permit the recording thereof or any memorandum thereof in the public real estate records of the jurisdiction in which any Building is located.

31. SURVIVAL.

Without limiting any other obligations which, by their terms, may survive the expiration or prior termination of the term of this Agreement, all obligations on the part of either party to indemnify, defend, or hold the other party harmless, as set forth herein (including, without limitation, Licensee's obligations under Sections 12.1 and 21.2) shall survive the expiration or prior termination of any such term.

32. BIND AND BENEFIT.

The terms and conditions contained herein shall inure to the benefit of and be binding upon Licensor and Licensee and each of their respective heirs, executors, administrators, successors, and permitted assigns.

33. ESTOPPEL.

Each party to this Agreement shall, upon fifteen (15) days' prior notice from the other party issued not more than two (2) times in any period of twelve (12) consecutive months, execute, acknowledge, and deliver to the requesting party a statement in writing (a) certifying that this Agreement is unmodified and in full force and effect (or, if modified, stating the nature of such modification and certifying that this Agreement, as so modified, is in full force and effect) and the date to which the Percentage Fee, the Minimum Fee, and other charges are paid, if any, and (b) acknowledging that there are not, to the certifying party's knowledge without any obligation to investigate, any uncured defaults on the part of the requesting party, or specifying such defaults if any are claimed.

34. ESTABLISHMENT OF CABLE DISTRIBUTION SYSTEM (CDS).

34.1 Notwithstanding any other provision in this Agreement, Licensor reserves the rights to install and operate a central telecommunications Cable Distribution System ("CDS") in the Building. The CDS may include a main cross-connect ("MC") for use by competitive service providers to reach tenant demarcation points in the Building. The MC shall serve as the minimum point of entry ("MPOE") demarcation point for service providers having access thereto. The MC shall also serve as the origination point of the CDS. The telephone closet demarcation block on each floor of the building will serve as the termination point of the CDS on that floor.

34.2 If Licensor installs a CDS:

(a) Licensee shall, at Licensee's expense, connect all new service and demarcation facilities (installed after the date of Licensor's CDS installation) to the CDS.

(b) Licensee shall utilize the CDS for providing all new Services (commenced after the date of Licensor's CDS installation) to Licensee's customers, once Licensor notifies Licensee that the MC is ready for service.

(c) Licensor may charge all competitive providers having access to the CDS (including Licensee) a fee for CDS access ("CDS Fee"), on a non-discriminatory basis (without exception), which fee will generally represent an economic benefit to Licensee over and above the Licensee's cost to install, maintain and manage a competing riser system.

(d) Notwithstanding any provision herein to the contrary, if Licensee installs any Equipment, Cable or conduit in the Building for the purpose of providing Services to tenants in the Building prior to the installation of the CDS, then Licensee shall have the right to keep and use such Equipment, cable and conduit in the Building until the end of the then current term, but Licensee shall utilize the CDS for Licensee's new customers in the Building.

34.3 Licensor shall repair or replace the CDS as necessary to eliminate any interruption or other adverse effects caused by malfunction, damage or destruction of the CDS, the cost of which shall be borne by Licensee if the problem was caused by the act or omission of Licensee, its agents, representatives, employees or invitees. In limitation of the foregoing, Licensor's obligation to repair or replace the CDS shall apply only to the extent necessary to reach premises in the Building that are used by tenants after the malfunction, damage or destruction or that, if damaged or destroyed, will be again used by tenants upon the completion of restoration or repair thereof.

34.4 In the event of malfunction of, damage to, or destruction of the CDS, as Licensee's sole remedies, (i) that the annual License Fee and CDS Fee paid by Licensee under the Agreement shall equitably abate (to the degree related to the defect) from the date of such malfunction, damage or destruction until the date upon which Licensor completes its repair or replacement of the CDS, or (ii) the right to utilize the Licensed Areas and Licensee's Equipment to service Licensee's customers in the Building in the same manner available to Licensee prior to Licensor's installation of the CDS. Licensor shall promptly provide to Licensee the phone number(s) for the person or persons responsible for the operation and maintenance of the CDS.

34.5 Except as otherwise provided in Section 35.4 above, in no event shall Licensee have any right to make any claim against Licensor for any damages whatsoever in connection with or arising from the CDS, including, without limitation, consequential damages in any such circumstance. Licensor may assign or delegate its rights and obligations under this Section 35 to another party which shall assume or accept in writing all of Licensor's obligations under this Section 35 arising from and after the date of such assignment or delegation (except with respect to Licensee's remedies under clauses 35.4(I) and 35.4(ii) above), provided that any such assignee shall further agree in writing to indemnify, defend and hold Licensee harmless from and against any claims or liability arising from any interruption or other adverse effects caused by malfunction, damage or destruction of the CDS, unless due to Licensee's gross negligence or willful misconduct.

35. REPRESENTATIONS AND COVENANTS FOR REIT LICENSORS.

Certain of Licensor's affiliates, including _____ Realty Trust, a _____ real estate investment trust, are treated as real estate investment trusts ("REITs") for federal income tax purposes. In connection with the REIT requirements that such affiliates must satisfy, including those requirements relating to sources of gross income, Licensee represents and covenants to Licensor as of the date hereof and continuing for the Term, for the benefit of Licensor and its affiliates (including _____ Realty Trust), that:

(a) all Services are provided by Licensee on a non-exclusive basis to Tenants and such Tenants are free to obtain such Services by or through other telecommunications providers;

(b) Licensee will not provide Services to Tenants that it does not offer to its other business customers;

(c) Licensee's Services will not be customized to fit the specific needs of a particular Tenant; however, Tenants will be offered a menu of Services by Licensee that are generally available to other customers of telecommunications providers; and Tenants may choose the Services they wish to receive from such menu;

(d) the Services provided by Licensee to Tenants will be services that are customarily rendered to Tenants of commercial office properties in the area where the Building is located.

(e) Licensee will not offer or provide any services at any Building other than the Services, unless (1) Licensee has obtained Licensor's prior written consent or (2) (i) Licensee has given Licensor at least two weeks prior written notice and (ii) Licensor has not given Licensee within such two week period a letter or other document from Licensor's tax counsel stating that there is a significant risk the offering of such services by Licensee would cause income received by Licensor from Licensee or any Tenant to fail to be "qualifying" income for purposes of Section 856 (c) (2) or 856 (c) (3) of the Internal Revenue Code of 1986, as amended.

36. SALE OR TRANSFER BY LICENSOR; BIND AND BENEFIT.

Upon the occurrence of a sale or other transfer of a Building during the Term of this Agreement, the purchaser or transferee of Licensor's interest in such Building shall assume in writing all of Licensor's covenants, agreements, rights and obligations under this Agreement and Licensor shall be released formed or satisfied hereunder with respect to such Building accruing after the effective date of such sale or transfer. The terms and conditions contained herein shall inure to the benefit of and be binding upon Licensor and Licensee and each of their respective heirs, executors, administrators, successors, and permitted assigns. This Agreement shall run with title to the Real Property and be binding upon any and all persons who subsequently acquire an interest in the Building(s) or Real Property.

IN WITNESS WHEREOF, the parties hereto have executed this Agreement as of the _____ day of _____, _____.

WITNESS: LICENSOR:

_____   _____

                                By: _____
                                Name: _____
                                Title: _____
                                Date: _____

                                ATTEST:

                                  By:

_____

                                Name: _____

                                WITNESS: LICENSEE:

_____   _____

                                By: _____
                                Name: _____
                                Title: _____
                                Date: _____

                                  ATTEST:

                                By: _____
                                Name: _____

EXHIBITS TO COMMUNICATIONS LICENSE AGREEMENT

EXHIBIT A—Land
EXHIBIT B—Building(s)
EXHIBIT C—Equipment Room Location
EXHIBIT D—Form of Subscription Agreement
SCHEDULE 1—Minimum Fee

Form Marketing Agreement

MARKETING AND COOPERATION AGREEMENT

This Marketing and Cooperation Agreement (this "Agreement") is made this ___ day of _____, _____ between _____, a _____ ("Owner") and _____, a _____("Provider").

BACKGROUND

A. Owner or one of its affiliates or clients is the record or beneficial owner of certain commercial buildings which are listed on Exhibit A attached hereto (the "Buildings");

B. Provider and Owner have agreed upon a form of telecommunications service agreement (the "Services Agreement") which is attached hereto as Exhibit B setting forth the terms and conditions on which Owner will provide access to the Buildings to Provider;

C. Under the terms of the Services Agreements, Provider desires to access the Buildings to install or have installed routers, switches, servers, cabling, data transmission lines and related equipment as more fully described on Exhibit ___ to each Services Agreement (the "Facilities") and provide internet access and network services, as more fully described on Exhibit ___ attached to each Services Agreement (the "Services") to tenants of the Buildings (the "Tenants"); and

D. In connection with Provider providing the Services to the Tenants pursuant to the terms hereof and each Services Agreement, Owner shall afford Provider certain rights and privileges under the terms and conditions of this Agreement.

TERMS

NOW, THEREFORE, in consideration of the mutual agreements set forth in this Agreement, and intending to be legally bound, the parties agree as set forth below:

1. Capitalized Terms. Each capitalized term used in this Agreement shall have the meaning ascribed to it in the Services Agreement form, unless otherwise defined herein.

2. Services Agreements. Provider shall give Owner at least ten (10) business days prior written notice of the scheduled commencement date for the Installation in a Building and, prior to such date, Owner shall enter (or cause the owner, if other than Owner of each Building to enter) into a Services Agreement with

Provider, and Provider shall enter into such Services Agreement with the Building owner.

3. Consideration to Owner.

In consideration for Owner permitting Provider to market and provide Telecommunication Services to the Tenants and to access the Buildings, Provider shall (i) pay Owner the Charge set forth in the Services Agreements and (ii) issue to Owner the Warrant contemporaneously with the execution of this Agreement to purchase [number to be determined based on calculation of _____ shares per million square feet of Building space] shares of Provider's Common Stock.

4. Marketing.

4.1   Provider's Rights and Obligations. Provider shall market the Services to the Tenants in accordance with the following:

4.1.1 Required Materials. Provider shall develop and print specialized marketing materials for each Building, for use in marketing the Services to Tenants of such Building (the "Required Materials") and shall provide copies of each to Owner in advance of any use or distribution. Owner may, in its reasonable discretion and upon written notice to Provider, reject the use of any such marketing materials. Upon receipt of such rejection, Provider shall abstain from using such materials. The Required Materials for each Building shall consist of (i) a printed color pamphlet that describes in reasonable detail the Services offered in such Building, (ii) a letter to each Tenant of such Building from Provider that introduces Provider and its Services to the Tenants, and (iii) such other written materials Provider may include, subject to Owner's approval.

4.1.2 Marketing Employees. Provider's marketing employees shall (i) distribute printed marketing materials to market Provider's Services to Tenants, (ii) assist and train Owner's personnel to aid Provider in the marketing of its Services to Tenants and prospective Tenants and (iii) attend leasing and marketing meetings with Owner's personnel and leasing agents in order to develop and implement cross marketing plans and strategies.

4.1.3 Marketing Standards. Provider shall only solicit customers in a professional and first class manner. The Required Materials and all other printed or on-line marketing materials used by Provider which (i) refer specifically to Owner or (ii) use any Owner Mark (as defined below) in any manner shall be subject to Owner's prior written approval. All such marketing shall indicate that Provider is responsible for the Services and that Owner is not in any way responsible for the Services.

4.1.4 Building Websites. During the Initial Term, Provider shall be designated the exclusive Website developer for each of the Buildings (which shall not include Tenants in the Buildings). Provider shall develop, host, maintain, service and periodically update a site on the world wide web portion of the Internet for each Building (each, a "Website"). Each Website will provide information to Tenants of the Building relating to the Building, Owner and the Services and other services that are available to Tenants, and shall be based upon Provider's then-current standard website ("Standard Website"). Provider shall seek Owner's input in advance of constructing each Website for material and information that Owner chooses to have included on the Website. Prior to making any Website available to the public or Tenants, Provider shall provide full access to such Website for review and reasonable approval by Owner. Provider shall make such modifications to Websites beyond the Standard Website as are reasonably requested by Owner; provided that, once initial construction of the Standard Website is completed, Provider may charge Owner all or part of the cost of any such requested modification which Provider reasonably deems to be primarily for Owner's benefit or otherwise unnecessary to delivery of the Services. However, if any modifications are for the benefit of Provider or any other third party, including Provider's other customers, Owner shall only pay its allocable portion of the cost. Provider shall maintain all records, including records in electronic form pertaining to each Website and domain name.

4.1.5 Milestone Schedule. The performance of the services required in connection with the Website shall be completed in accordance with the description of services to provided and the time frame set forth in the "Milestone Schedule" attached hereto as Exhibit E, provided that Owner shall have delivered to Provider all information and materials deemed reasonably necessary or appropriate by Provider, all in a timely fashion and in any event not later than ten (10) days next following Provider's request therefor, failing which Provider's performance obligations which are dependent in whole or in part upon Provider's receipt of such information and materials in the form specified shall be extended an identical period of time to reflect such delay by Owner in providing such information and materials. Exhibit E also shall contain the requirements for the development of the Website, including operational and functional capabilities and performance requirements (the "Specifications"). Owner shall have ten (10) days to inspect and test each such product produced by Provider (each a "Deliverable") to determine if it reasonably conforms to the Specifications. Each Deliverable shall be deemed to be accepted, unless Owner provides written notice stating the defect in reasonable detail within the time frame set forth above. Provider shall then have thirty (30) days to remedy such failure and redeliver such Deliverable to Owner for its approval, such process of submission and review shall be repeated until each Deliverable reasonably conforms to its

Specifications, provided, however, that in no event shall the Milestone Schedule be deemed to be breached in any manner while such process of submission and review shall be ongoing provided that Provider is seeking to conform all Deliverables with reasonable diligence. Except in instances of an extension pursuant to a Force Majeure as set forth in Section 10.1 below or in the case of an extension pursuant to delays caused by Owner as set forth above or in such instance as the parties shall be engaged in the process of review and resubmission as above, a failure by Provider to provide Deliverables to Owner within the agreed upon time period as set forth in Exhibit E (subject to notice and cure period as provided above) shall void the exclusivity of Provider's Website developer status for each Building actually affected by such failure.

4.1.6 Revenue Sharing.

4.1.6.1 Any revenue, income or payment received or derived by Owner from the sale of advertising through the Website ("Advertising Revenue") and any revenue, income or payment derived from e-commerce transactions through the Website, including transaction fees derived from the sale of goods and/or services ("E-Commerce Revenue") shall be payable to Provider as follows: (1) If the goods are sold to or services are rendered to a particular industry or service market developed by Owner or if the advertising is sold by Owner, then Provider shall receive five percent (5%) of the resulting gross Advertising Revenue and E-Commerce Revenue; (2) If the goods are sold to or services are rendered to a particular industry or service market developed jointly by both Owner and Provider or if the advertising is sold by both Owner and Provider, then Provider shall receive fifty percent (50%) of the resulting gross Advertising Revenue and E-Commerce Revenue.

4.1.6.2 Within thirty (30) days following the close of each calendar quarter for so long as Owner is paid or owed cash or consideration on which Provider is entitled to a share of the Advertising Revenue and/or E-Commerce Revenue, as provided above, Owner shall pay Provider all amounts due for such quarter and shall submit with each payment a statement providing in reasonable detail the basis for such payment.

4.1.6.3 Provider shall have the right to inspect and audit the books and records of Owner for the purpose of verifying any reports, information and payment due to Provider under this Agreement. The acceptance by Provider of payments of Advertising Revenue and E-Commerce Revenue shall be without prejudice to Provider's right to an examination of Owner's books and records. In the event of any shortfall in payment to Provider is found which exceeds five percent (5%) of the total due to Provider for the reporting period audited, Owner shall promptly pay to Provider any deficiency in Advertising Revenue and E-Commerce Revenue due to Provider and reimburse Provider for all the costs incurred by Provider in connection with the audit, together with interest at Interest Rate based on a 365 day year, compounded annually.

4.1.7 Website Identity Ownership. Each Website domain name, URL and viewsource code and all of the Owner Information (as defined below) included in such Website (together, the "Website Identity") shall be considered "works made for hire" (as defined in Section 101 of the U.S. Copyright Act in effect as of the date hereof, notwithstanding any changes or amendments which may hereafter be made thereto), shall become at the instant of creation or expression the sole property of Owner, and Provider shall retain no rights or interest of any kind in any Website Identity, except as specifically provided in this Agreement and the Services Agreements. In the event that, by operation or law or otherwise, Provider shall retain any rights to any Website Identity, other than under this Agreement or a Services Agreement Provider hereby waives, and transfers and assigns to Owner, without further consideration, all of such right, title and interest in and to such Website Identity, including any moral rights. To the extent any right, title or interest in and to any Website Identity cannot lawfully be assigned by Provider to Owner or one or more of its designees, Provider hereby grants to Owner an exclusive, royalty-free, transferable, irrevocable, perpetual, worldwide license (with rights to sublicense) to use, exploit and practice such nonassignable right, title and interest. To the extent any right, title or interest in and to any Website Identity can neither be lawfully assigned nor licensed by Provider to Owner or one or more of its designees, Provider hereby irrevocably waives and agrees never to assert such nonassignable and nonlicensable right, title or interest against Owner or any of its affiliates or clients or any of Owner's, its affiliates' or clients' successors in interest. As used herein, "Owner Information" means all information which specifically identifies, describes or relates to Owner, Tenants or any Building, including the Owner Marks. This Section 4.1.7 shall survive termination of this Agreement.

4.1.8 Website Contents Ownership. Except for the Website Identity, Provider (or, as applicable, Provider's vendors and licensors) shall have and retain all rights, title and interest to the contents of each Website and all related Intellectual Property (as defined below) of whatever kind, including, without limitation, web portals, web links and other linked Websites owned by or licensed to Provider, applications, trade names and trademarks (including, without limitation, "Eureka" and "Eureka Broadband"), service marks, copyright materials, and concepts, designs and techniques developed or used in the construction of the Websites (altogether, "Provider's Intellectual Property"). Owner acknowledges that it neither has nor, by reason of this Agreement or the

Services Agreements or any activity pursuant hereto or thereto, will acquire any rights, title or interest in any of Provider's Intellectual Property; and Owner hereby irrevocably waives and agrees never to assert any claim, right, title or interest in any such property against Provider or any of its affiliates or successors in interest. As used herein, "Intellectual Property" means patent rights, copyrights, trade secrets, trademarks, trade names, service marks, moral rights, know-how and any other similar rights or intangible assets recognized under any laws or international conventions, and in any country or jurisdiction in the world, as intellectual creations to which rights of ownership accrue, and all registrations, applications, disclosures, renewals, extensions, continuations or reissues of the foregoing now or hereafter in force. This Section 4.1.8 shall survive termination of this Agreement.

4.1.9 Website Transition. In the event that this Agreement is terminated with respect to the Websites for any reason, Provider agrees that it will continue to host, maintain and service each Website in accordance with the terms of this Agreement for a period of up to six (6) months following such termination. During such six-month period, Provider will cooperate with Owner to transition each Website to another provider (which may be Owner) designated by Owner in its sole discretion that will host, maintain, service and update each Website. Provider will provide to Owner or its designee all source and object code relating to each Website and all other written materials or computer code developed by Provider that is useful in the hosting, maintaining, servicing or updating any Website; provided, however, that Provider shall have the right to modify the Websites and such codes in a professional manner so as to remove any or all of Provider's Intellectual Property. This Section 4.1.9 shall survive termination of this Agreement. Further, Provider shall provide to Subscribers reasonable cooperation in the course of transition from Provider to another Services provider upon the expiration or earlier termination of this Agreement or the applicable subscription agreement.

4.1.10 Provider Personnel. Provider shall maintain a staff of three (3) qualified and experienced employees per 1.5 million square feet of Building space to operate and maintain the Facilities, and ensure delivery of the Services, in a first class manner. Such Provider representatives shall provide: (1) tenant interface for problem resolution and customer change orders; (2) interface with third party telecommunications companies requiring access to Provider's Facilities within the Building; and (3) support services to the Owner and property manager, if any, as may be reasonably necessary.

4.2   Obligations of Owner. Owner shall provide the following benefits and privileges to Provider in order to further Provider's marketing efforts to Tenants for Services:

4.2.1 Marketing. Upon the completion of the Installation for each Building, or such earlier time as Provider may reasonably request, Owner will distribute to each Tenant of such Building a letter from Owner introducing Provider to such Tenant and enclosing Provider's Required Materials (which will be supplied by Provider at Provider's sole expense). Owner will include a substantially similar letter and the Required Materials in its standard package of materials that it sends to prospective Tenants for such Building. Owner shall display the Required Materials in the management office of the Buildings for which Installation has been completed, which materials will be supplied to Owner by Provider at Provider's sole expense.

4.2.2 Events, Signage and Advertising. Provider may sponsor marketing events at the Buildings at its sole cost and expense. Provider shall provide to Owner a general description of such event(s) which shall include a description of the time, location and theme and which shall be provided monthly (or for some other reasonable period) in advance and which may be provided as a list or schedule of all such then anticipated events. Such events shall be subject to Owner's prior approval. Provider shall be permitted to place a sign, subject to Owner's prior approval as to size, content, design and location, in the lobby of each Building for which Installation has been substantially completed. Provider may place advertisements in local newspapers and trade magazines introducing Provider's Services within the Buildings, subject to Owner's prior approval. Provider may install a specialized "wall jack" in each Tenant space with the consent of the Tenant and subject to the terms and conditions of the Services Agreements.

4.2.3 Protection of Owner's Rights. Notwithstanding anything in this Agreement to the contrary (i) Owner may confer any rights or entitlements (other than those expressly reserved to Provider in this Agreement) upon any other provider of telecommunications services similar to or the same as the Services, (ii) any Tenant may obtain telecommunication services from a provider other than Provider, (iii) Owner may enter into other arrangements with a provider of telecommunications services, other than Provider, (iv) Owner shall not make any representation or warranty to Tenants as to the quality of Provider's Services (and Owner will specifically indicate in its correspondence with Tenants that no such representation or warranty is given), and (v) Owner will not be liable in any respect whatsoever for any services provided by Provider to any Tenant or in connection with, related to or arising from the development, hosting, maintaining, servicing or updating of the Websites.

4.2.4 Tenant Information. At such time as Provider is authorized hereunder to begin marketing the Services to Tenants of a Building, Owner shall provide Provider with a list to the extent such information is available (which Owner shall update for Provider not less than quarterly) of the name, suite number, contact telephone number, lease expiration date and renewal options for each Tenant in the Building (unless such disclosure to Provider is prohibited under any applicable lease). Owner shall also provide to Provider a list of names and contact telephone numbers for each property manager and building engineer of the Buildings. Provider shall keep such information confidential and Provider shall utilize such confidential information only for the purpose of attempting to market the Services in accordance with the terms hereof and shall not disclose, or permit disclosure of, such confidential information, except to agents and subcontractors retained by Provider in furtherance of this Agreement who have agreed to maintain such information in confidence and not to disclose or permit disclosure to any other person or entity whatsoever. Provider shall also take such other actions as may be necessary to prevent unauthorized use or disclosure of such confidential information in its possession or in the possession of such agents and subcontractors. Upon the termination of this Agreement, Provider will return to Owner or, at Owner's direction, destroy all records and documents containing such confidential information, including all copies thereof.

4.2.5 Meetings. Owner shall give Provider reasonable advance notice of, and permit Provider's designee to attend, any meetings or portions of meetings with or presentations to Tenants or prospective Tenants at which the provision of the Services is to be a material item of discussion or presentation. From time to time, upon Provider's reasonable requests, Owner shall cooperate with Provider in arranging meetings with or presentations to Tenants and prospective Tenants, either individually or in groups, for purposes of promoting the Services.

4.2.6 Office Space. To the extent reasonably practicable and subject to availability, Owner shall provide to Provider office space in certain of the Buildings, at reasonable rental rates as mutually agreed upon by Owner and Provider not to exceed forty dollars and 00/100 ($40.00) per square foot, and to be used for the sole purpose of Provider's performing its obligations and exercising its rights under this Agreement or the Services Agreements.

4.3 Trademark License.

4.3.1 License of Owner Trademarks. Owner hereby grants to Provider a non-exclusive royalty-free license during the term of this Agreement to use the trademarks and service marks of Owner listed on Exhibit D hereto in the precise form of the camera-ready proofs attached thereto (the "Owner Marks") for the sole purpose of marketing and promoting the Services to Tenants under this Agreement and in compliance with all of the terms and conditions of this Agreement. Provider shall comply with any written conditions imposed by Owner, as may be amended from time to time, with respect to the style, color, appearance and manner of use of the Owner Marks. Provider shall maintain a commercially reasonable standard of quality for all of its marketing and promotional materials. Provider acknowledges and agrees that (i) the Owner Marks are and shall remain the sole property of Owner, (ii) nothing in this Agreement shall convey to Provider any right of ownership in the Owner Marks, (iii) Provider shall not now or in the future contest the validity of any Owner Marks and (iv) Provider shall not knowingly take any action that would impair the value of or the goodwill associated with the Owner Marks. Provider acknowledges and agrees that all use of the Owner Marks shall inure to the benefit of Owner.

4.3.2 License of Provider Trademarks. Provider hereby grants to Owner a non-exclusive royalty-free license during the term of this Agreement to use the U.S. trademarks and service marks of Provider listed in Exhibit C hereto in the form of the camera-ready proofs attached thereto (the "Provider Marks") for the sole purpose of marketing and promoting the Services to Tenants under this Agreement and in compliance with all of the terms and conditions of this Agreement. Owner shall comply with any written conditions imposed by Provider, as may be amended from time to time, with respect to the style, color, appearance and manner of use of the Provider Marks. Owner shall maintain a standard of quality for the marketing and promotional materials commensurate with standards achieved and maintained by Provider. Owner acknowledges and agrees that (i) the Provider Marks are and shall remain the sole property of Provider, (ii) nothing in this Agreement shall convey to Owner any right of ownership in the Provider Marks, (iii) Owner shall not now or in the future contest the validity of any Provider Marks and (iv) Owner shall not take any action that would impair the value of or the goodwill associated with the Provider Marks. Owner acknowledges and agrees that all use of the Provider Marks shall inure to the benefit of Provider.

4.3.3 Indemnification against Infringement Claims. Each of Owner and Provider shall hold harmless, indemnify and defend the other, its partners, shareholders, directors, officers, employees and agents from and against any claims or liability for infringement of a third party's alleged rights in any of the indemnifying party's Marks, and related expenses (including attorneys' fees actually and reasonably incurred), arising out of the use of any such Marks by the indemnified party pursuant to and in accordance with the applicable provisions of this Agreement.

5. Provider Services. Provider shall perform its obligations under this Agreement and under each Services Agreement in a safe and first-class workmanlike manner and in accordance with all applicable laws and regulations.

In each of the Buildings, Provider shall be required to comply with the following in providing its Services, operating its Facilities and handling failures or problems with such equipment or services:

5.1   Quality of Services. Provider shall, at all times during the term hereof and during the term of each Services Agreement, use commercially reasonable efforts to meet the highest quality standards of the industry while providing the Services to the Tenants at a commercially reasonable and competitive price. During the term hereof Provider shall at its own cost, operate, maintain, repair, replace and periodically upgrade the Facilities. Further, Provider shall make commercially reasonable, good faith efforts to maintain modern and effective high speed Internet connections and other improvements related to the scope, nature and quality of the Services as technology is improved, and to maintain access speeds which are competitive with the market for Internet services.

5.2   Additional Services. Owner may from time to time request that Provider provide in any Building one or more telecommunication services not then currently being offered by Provider to Tenants of such Building but that are then being offered by other telecommunications providers in the metropolitan area in which the Building is located (or being marketed for introduction in such metropolitan area). If Provider does not, within thirty (30) days after receipt of a written request from Owner, agree to provide such non-offered services in such Building on a timetable and basis reasonably acceptable to Owner, Owner shall have the right, at its option to contract for such additional services from another telecommunications provider. Provider shall have the right to charge Tenants a competitive price or fee for any such additional services.

5.3   Technicians. Provider shall employ sufficient and qualified personnel to handle customer requests and complaints between the hours of 8 a.m. and 6 p.m. Monday through Friday, excepting legal holidays. Provider shall maintain a network operations center that will monitor the Facilities and Services 24 hours a day, seven days a week.

5.4   Notice of Owner's Non-Responsibility. Upon commencement of any Services to a Subscriber, Provider shall communicate to such Subscriber and such Subscriber shall acknowledge in writing in effect that (i) the Facilities and Services are being provided and maintained by Provider and not Owner, (ii) Owner has no responsibility or liability for the installation, operation, maintenance, use, repair or replacement of the Facilities, or the provision, quality or sufficiency of the Services, and (iii) by subscribing to and accepting the Services, Tenant agrees to release Owner from any such liability.

5.5   Tenant Complaint System. Provider shall develop a complaint processing system for the Tenants that subscribe to the Provider's Services. Such system shall include a contact telephone number, a processing and logging system to track system problems, Provider's response times and the resolution of all complaints.

5.6   Understandings Between the Parties. Provider will be solely responsible for billing and collections for the Provider's Services. Provider will be solely responsible for performing its own evaluations of the financial responsibility, creditworthiness and character of each Tenant. Provider agrees that Owner has expressly disclaimed any knowledge or warranty with respect to the financial condition of any Tenant and that Provider is proceeding at its own risk in entering into Subscription Agreements with Tenants and performing Services for Tenants. Owner shall have no responsibility for, or obligation or liability with respect to, (i) the quality, suitability, reliability or operation of the Facilities or Services, (ii) compliance with applicable laws and regulations with respect thereto, or (iii) the compatibility of the Provider's equipment with the heating, ventilation, air conditioning, plumbing, electrical, fire protection, safety, security, public utility or other systems at the Buildings. Provider does not rely on the fact, nor does Owner represent, that any specific Tenant or type or number of Tenants shall, during the term of this Agreement, or any renewals or extensions thereof, occupy space in any of the Buildings.

5.7   Compliance with Laws; Permits; Regulatory Actions. In its performance of this Agreement and each Services Agreement, each of Owner and Provider, and anyone acting on such party's behalf or at its expense (including its independent contractors, employees and agents), shall comply with all municipal, county, state, federal and other governmental body laws, ordinances and regulations, including without limitation, Federal Communications Commission rules and regulations applicable to such party or its performance of this Agreement and each Services Agreement ("Applicable Laws"). In its performance of this Agreement and each Services Agreement, Provider and anyone acting on its behalf or at its expense (including its independent contractors, employees and agents) will obtain and maintain all permits, licenses regulatory approvals and authorizations which may be required under any Applicable Law ("Permits") for installation, operating and maintenance of the Facilities and provision of the Services, and Owner and anyone acting on its behalf or at its expense (including its independent contractors, employees and agents) will obtain and maintain all Permits required for the occupancy of the Buildings and operation of Building power and mechanical systems generally. Upon the request of Owner, Provider shall make all of its Permits, and all correspondence with government agencies with respect thereto, available to Owner for inspection and copying. Provider shall promptly notify Owner if it becomes aware that any aspect of its performance of this Agreement or any Services Agreement is being investigated by any federal, state or local agency, if any of its Permits is suspended or revoked or expires or if any federal, state and/or local agency takes any action which prevents Provider from performing under this Agreement and each

Services Agreement in full compliance with the terms hereof and thereof. Provider shall inform Owner of legal or regulatory developments at the Federal and State level of which Provider is aware and which it believes likely to impair Provider's ability to provide the Services.

5.8   Nature of Services. Except as otherwise provided in the Services Agreements, (i) Provider shall not provide any services to Tenants unless such services are also available to such Tenants from other telecommunications service providers, (ii) Provider shall not provide any services to any Tenant that it does not also provide to other customers who are not Tenants, (iii) any services provided by Provider to a Tenant will not be customized to fit the specific needs of such Tenant, (iv) this Agreement is a bona fide agreement, negotiated at arm's length between Owner and Provider, and is of a type customarily entered into by landlords and service providers in the geographic area in which the Buildings are located, (v) the services offered or provided by Provider to Tenants, will be selected by Tenants from a menu of services, all of which are generally available to other customers of Provider and (vi) Provider shall not provide any services to Tenants of a Building unless such services are of the type which are customarily rendered to tenants of commercial office properties in the geographic areas in which that Building is located.

6. Provider Reporting.

6.1   Installation Reporting. Prior to the time that the Installation has been completed for each Building, Provider shall provide to Owner no less than five (5) days after the end of each calendar month, a written report as of the last day of the previous month detailing (i) the status of Provider's progress with respect to the Installation in each Building, including dates on which Installation is expected to commence and progress with respect to Buildings for which Installation is in progress but has not been completed, and (ii) the status of provisioning wide area network circuits for each Building, including circuits ordered and the expected timing of the provisioning of circuits.

6.2   Operations Reporting. Provider shall provide to Owner no less than ten (10) business days after the end of each calendar quarter, a written report as of the last day of the previous calendar quarter detailing: (i) Provider sales and marketing efforts at each Building, (ii) Tenants that have subscribed to the Provider's services and a report summarizing all revenue and usage associated with each Tenant's use of Services, (iii) any problems or complaints that Provider has encountered in its marketing of the Services to the Tenants, along with any other information that would be relevant with respect to Provider's activities at the Buildings.

7. Indemnity.

7.1.1 By Provider. Provider shall indemnify, defend, and hold harmless the Owner, its partners, shareholders, members, agents, consultants, employees, officers, directors, clients (as record Owner of a Building), affiliates and lenders (collectively "Owner Affiliates") against any third-party liabilities, damages, losses, actions, causes of actions, expenses, costs, injuries, disputes or claims (including legal fees) incurred by Owner or Owner Affiliates arising out of: (i) any default in the performance of Provider's obligations under this Agreement or any Services Agreement provided such failure was not caused by Owner's gross negligence or willful misconduct, (ii) any malfeasance on the part of Provider or its employees, invitees, servants or agents, (iii) any acts of Provider or Provider's employees or agents beyond the scope of Provider's authority under this Agreement not authorized or ratified by Owner, (iv) delivery or offering of (or any interruption in or failure to deliver or offer) the Websites or Services including but not limited to any claim or liability incurred by a Tenant in connection with related to or arising from the delivery of the Services or Websites or any interruption in or failure to deliver or offer the Services or the Websites, (v) Provider's maintenance of the Facilities or failure to do the same, (vi) infringement or misappropriation of an Intellectual Property right of a third party in connection with the Websites, Services and Facilities, except where arising from the use of Owner's Marks in compliance with this Agreement, (vii) Owner's use of Provider's Marks or other Provider Intellectual Property in compliance with this Agreement, and (viii) breach of the representations and warranties of Provider set forth in Section _____ of the Services Agreement.

7.1.2 By Owner. Owner shall indemnify, defend, and hold harmless the Provider, its partners, shareholders, members, agents, consultants, employees, officers, directors, and lenders (collectively "Provider Affiliates") against any liabilities, damages, losses, or claims (including actual and reasonable legal fees) incurred by Provider or Provider Affiliates arising out of: (i) any default in the performance of Owner's obligations under this Agreement provided such failure was not caused by Provider's gross negligence or willful misconduct, (ii) any malfeasance on the part of Owner or its employees or agents, (iii) any acts of Owner or Owner's employees or agents beyond the scope of Owner's authority under this Agreement not authorized or ratified by Provider, (iv) Provider's use of Owner's Marks in compliance with this Agreement, and (viii) breach of the representations and warranties of Owner set forth in Section 11 of the Services Agreement.

7.1.3 Survival. The provisions of this Section 7 shall survive termination of this Agreement.

8. Confidentiality.

8.1   Except as may be required by applicable governmental laws, rules or regulations or as may be otherwise be agreed in writing by the parties, no party will disclose the terms and conditions hereof or of any Services Agreement or any Confidential Information (as defined below) exchanged between them as a result of this Agreement, without the prior written consent of the other party. Notwithstanding the foregoing, either party may disclose the terms of this Agreement, or any Services Agreement (i) to its employees, agents or professional advisors on a "need to know" basis solely for the purposes of carrying out its obligations under this Agreement provided that such parties are obligated to the disclosing party to maintain the confidentiality of such matters, (ii) where required to do so by law or court order, and (iii) as reasonably necessary to enforce such party's rights hereunder (provided that, before disclosing any Confidential Information pursuant to clause (ii) or (iii) above, the disclosing party shall notify the other party as much in advance as circumstances reasonably permit). For purposes of this Agreement, "Confidential Information" means (a) all information that either party furnishes to the other party on or after the date of this Agreement, which such party designates as proprietary or confidential by use of a legend, label or similar designation, (b) with respect to oral information, all such information that either party states is to be proprietary or confidential and (c) all information that should reasonably be considered proprietary or confidential. The parties expressly agree that all information relating to the Installation and the usage by Tenants of the Services shall be deemed to be Confidential Information of both Parties. Any information provided by Owner to Provider hereof and any information relating to the Buildings or prospective Tenants which is provided by Owner to Provider hereunder or which Provider learns in its performance of this Agreement and the Services Agreements shall be deemed to be Confidential Information of Owner. Notwithstanding the foregoing, however, Confidential Information shall not include any information which is or become generally known publicly or is discovered by a party from public sources.

8.2   Each party shall treat and hold the Confidential Information in confidence and shall protect the confidentiality thereof in the same manner in which it protects the confidentiality of similar information and data of its own (at all times exercising at least a reasonable degree of care in the protection of Confidential Information).

8.3   The obligations under this Section 8 shall survive the expiration or termination of this Agreement for a period of five (5) years after the expiration or termination of this Agreement.

8.4   All Confidential Information which may be furnished to a party shall continue to be the property of the party furnishing the same.

8.5   Except as expressly provided in this Agreement, no rights or licenses, express or implied, are hereby granted to any Confidential Information, including without limitation, any patents, trademarks, service marks, trade names, copyrights or trade secrets, as a result of or related to this Agreement.

9. Notices. All notices, demands, waivers and other communications required or permitted by this Agreement, together with all documents and materials required hereunder, shall in each case be in writing (whether or not a writing is expressly required hereby), and shall be delivered: (i) by courier or hand delivery, or (ii) by United States Mail, sent by certified mail, return receipt requested, postage prepaid, or (iii) by Federal Express or another nationally recognized express delivery service, or (iv) by facsimile and all such deliveries shall be made or sent to the following addresses (or to such other address as a party may hereafter designate for itself by notice to the other party):

9.1 If to Provider:

Attention:

With copy to:

9.2 If to Owner:

Attention:

With copy to:

and shall be deemed given and received (A) if delivered or transmitted before 5:00 pm recipient's local time on a business day, or if tendered for delivery between the hours 9:00 am and 5:00 pm recipient's local time on a business day and refused, then on the date of actual (or refused) delivery or actual transmission as evidenced by postal or courier receipt (or by a completed transmission log sheet generated by the sending telecopier) and (B) otherwise, on the business day next following the date of actual delivery or transmission; provided, however, that any communication delivered by fax must be confirmed within three business days by duplicate notice delivered as otherwise provided herein.

10.   Miscellaneous.

10.1 Force Majeure. The time period for a party to fulfill any obligation or satisfy any condition on its part to be performed or satisfied under this

Agreement shall be extended one day for each day that such party is delayed in the performance or satisfaction thereof by any cause which is beyond such party's reasonable ability to control, including (without limitation) acts of God or the State, war, civil commotion, strikes or other labor unrest, unavailability of telecommunications capacity not caused by such party and any breach of the provisions of this Agreement by the other party, or other unjustified act or failure to act, on the part of the other party (including, without limitation, the other party's failure to respond in timely fashion to requests for approval or consent). In order to claim the benefits of this Section 10.1 for any such delay, though, the party invoking this Section must give the other party notice of the delay and its cause within ten (10) business days after such delay begins.

10.2 Time of Essence. Time is of the essence of this Agreement and each of its provisions.

10.3 Attorney's Fees. The prevailing party shall be entitled to reasonable attorney's fees incurred in connection with the institution of any action or proceeding in court to enforce any provision hereof or for damages by reason of any alleged breach or default of any provision of this Agreement or for a declaration of either party's rights or obligations hereunder or for any other judicial remedy, at law or in equity.

10.4 Governing Law. This Agreement will be governed by and subject to, and construed in accordance with, the internal laws of the State of New York without giving effect to the choice or conflict of laws provisions thereof.

10.5 Waiver of Trial by Jury. Each of Provider and the Owner waives any right to trial by jury in any action, proceeding or counterclaim (whether based upon contract, tort or otherwise) seeking specific performance of any provision of this Agreement, for damages for any breach under this Agreement, or otherwise for enforcement of any right or remedy hereunder.

10.6 Further Assurances. The parties hereto covenant and agree that they will execute such other and further instruments and documents as are or may be reasonably necessary to effectuate and carry out the purpose and intent of this Agreement.

10.7 Parties in Interest. This Agreement will be binding upon and inure solely to the benefit of the parties hereto, their respective successors, legal representatives, heirs and assigns as permitted under this Agreement, and no other person will have or be construed to have any legal or equitable right, remedy or claim under or in respect of, or by virtue of, this Agreement or any provision contained herein.

10.8 Publicity. No party shall issue any publicity or press release regarding the contractual relationship hereunder or under any Services Agreement or regarding the parties' activities hereunder or under any Services Agreement without obtaining the prior written approval and consent to such publicity or releases from the other party hereto, which written approval and consent will not be unreasonably withheld.

10.9 Independent Contractor. The parties to this Agreement are independent contractors. Neither party is an agent, representative or partner of the other party. Neither party shall have any right, power or authority to enter into any agreement for or on behalf of, or incur any obligation or liability of, or to otherwise bind, the other party. This Agreement shall not be interpreted or construed to create an association, agency, joint venture or partnership between the parties or to impose any liability attributable to such a relationship upon either party.

10.10 Headings. The headings preceding the text of the sections and subsections hereof are inserted solely for convenience of reference and shall not constitute a part of this Agreement, nor shall they affect its meaning, construction or effect.

10.11 Severability. To the extent any provision of this Agreement shall be invalid or unenforceable, it will be considered deleted herefrom and the remainder of such provision and of this Agreement will be unaffected and will continue in full force and effect.

10.12 Counterpart Execution. This Agreement may be executed by facsimile and in counterparts, each of which will be deemed an original and all of which when taken together will constitute one and the same instrument.

10.13 Entire Agreement; Amendments. This Agreement, the Warrant and the Services Agreements set forth all of the promises, covenants, agreements, conditions and undertakings between the parties hereto with respect to the subject matter hereof, and supersedes all prior and contemporaneous agreements and understandings, inducements or conditions, express or implied, oral or written, except as contained herein. This Agreement may not be changed orally but only by an agreement in writing, duly executed by or on behalf of the party against whom enforcement of any waiver, change, modification, consent or discharge is sought.

10.14 No Waiver. The failure of either party to insist upon or enforce strict performance by the other party of any provision of this Agreement or to exercise any right under this Agreement shall not be construed as a waiver or relinquishment to any extent of such party's right to assert or rely upon any such provision or right in that or any other instance; rather, the same shall be and remain in full force and effect.

10.15 Assignment. Provider shall not assign, transfer, mortgage, pledge, hypothecate, or encumber (including by way of merger, consolidation or sale of more than twenty five percent (25%) of Provider's stock or assets) this Agreement or any Services Agreement without first securing the written consent of Owner in Owner's sole and absolute discretion, except that (i) any public offering of Provider's stock, and the trading of Provider's stock on any public exchange or in any public securities market, shall not be deemed an assignment of this Agreement; (ii) Provider shall have the right to assign this Agreement to any entity which acquires all or substantially all of Provider's assets (whether by merger, consolidation, purchase or otherwise) without Owner's consent, so long as (x) such assignee assumes all of Provider's obligations and liabilities hereunder and (y) such assignee has a net worth which is at least equal to the greater of (a) Provider's net worth at the time of such assignment or (b) $50 million; and (iii) if a proposed assignment is solely in connection with a corporate financing or internal reorganization of Provider and Provider's assignee assumes all of Provider's obligations and liabilities hereunder, Owner's consent shall be required but shall not be unreasonably withheld. Any permitted assignment by Provider as described herein shall release Provider of its obligations hereunder. Owner shall the right to assign its rights and obligations under this Agreement as they relate to one or more of the Buildings, without securing the consent of Provider, in conjunction with Owner's (or its affiliates) sale or other disposition of such Buildings, or to the holder of any current or prospective mortgage or deed of trust or ground lessor as additional security or to lenders in connection with a financing related to a Building or Property or to any subsidiary or affiliate of Owner; but otherwise Owner shall not assign or otherwise transfer this Agreement without first securing the written consent of Provider in Provider's reasonable discretion. Any such assignment or other disposition by Owner shall release Owner of its obligations hereunder (as they relate to such Buildings) and Provider shall then look solely to such successor in interest of Owner (or its affiliates) in the Buildings for the performance of such obligations. Any purported assignment not in accordance with this Section 10.15 shall be void and of no effect as to the other party and, at the other party's sole option, shall be treated as an Event of Default.

10.16 Neither Owner nor Provider shall be liable for any incidental or consequential damages or special losses arising from any breach, failure to perform or termination of this Agreement or any Services Agreement whether foreseeable or not (except to the extent caused by such party's gross negligence or willful misconduct), and (b) entitled to any equitable relief or specific performance with respect to the performance or forbearance of any obligation of the other party.

IN WITNESS WHEREOF, the parties have caused this Agreement to be duly executed as of the date first written above.

OWNER:

By: _____
Name: _____
Title:_____
Date: _____

PROVIDER:

By: _____
Name: _____
Title:_____
Date: _____

EXHIBITS TO MARKETING AGREEMENT

Exhibit A—List of Buildings and Square Footage
Exhibit B—Form Services Agreement
Exhibit C—Provider Marks
Exhibit D—Owner Marks
Exhibit E—Milestone Schedule

INDEX